Understanding 12–14-Year-Olds

Understanding Your Child Series

The Tavistock Clinic has an international reputation as a centre of excellence for training, clinical mental health work, research and scholarship. Written by professionals working in the Child and Family and the Adolescent Departments, the guides in this series present balanced and sensitive advice that will help adults to become, or to feel that they are, "good enough" parents. Each book concentrates on a key transition in a child's life from birth to adolescence, looking especially at how parents' emotions and experiences interact with those of their children. The titles in the Understanding Your Child series are essential reading for new and experienced parents, relatives, friends and carers, as well as for the multi-agency professionals who are working to support children and their families.

other titles in the series

Understanding Your Baby
Sophie Boswell
ISBN 978 1 84310 242 7

Understanding Your One-Year-Old
Sarah Gustavus Jones
ISBN 978 1 84310 241 0

Understanding Your Two-Year-Old
Lisa Miller
ISBN 978 1 84310 288 5

Understanding Your Three-Year-Old
Louise Emanuel
ISBN 978 1 84310 243 4

Understanding 4–5-Year-Olds
Lesley Maroni
ISBN 978 1 84310 534 3

Understanding 6–7-Year-Olds
Corinne Aves
ISBN 978 1 84310 467 4

Understanding 12–14-Year-Olds
Margot Waddell
ISBN 978 1 84310 367 7

Understanding Your Young Child with Special Needs
Pamela Bartram
ISBN 978 1 84310 533 6

Understanding
12–14-Year-Olds

Margot Waddell

Jessica Kingsley Publishers
London and Philadelphia

First published in 2005
by Jessica Kingsley Publishers
116 Pentonville Road
London N1 9JB, UK
and
400 Market Street, Suite 400
Philadelphia, PA 19106, USA

www.jkp.com

Library of Congress Cataloging in Publication Data
Waddell, Margot, 1946-
Understanding 12-14-year-olds / Margot Waddell.
p. cm. -- (Understanding your child)
Includes bibliographical references and index.
ISBN-13: 978-1-84310-367-7 (pbk.)
ISBN-10: 1-84310-367-2 (pbk.)
1. Adolescence. 2. Teenagers. 3. Preteens. 4. Parent and teenager. I. Title: Understanding twelve-fourteen-year olds. II. Title. III. Understanding your child series.
HQ796.W13 2005
649'.125--dc22

2005005197

British Library Cataloguing in Publication Data
A CIP catalogue record for this book is available from the British Library

ISBN 978 1 84310 367 7

Printed and bound in Great Britain by
MPG Books Group, Cornwall

Contents

Acknowledgements

With heartfelt thanks to all those who have, directly or indirectly, contributed to this book: to family, friends, parents, teachers, patients and, above all, to the many young people who have shared their experiences and views with me so helpfully and generously.

Foreword

The Tavistock Clinic has an international reputation as a centre of excellence for training, clinical mental health work, research and scholarship. Established in 1920, its history is one of groundbreaking work. The original aim of the Clinic was to offer treatment which could be used as the basis of research into the social prevention and treatment of mental health problems, and to teach these emerging skills to other professionals. Later work turned towards the treatment of trauma, the understanding of conscious and unconscious processes in groups, as well as important and influential work in developmental psychology. Work in perinatal bereavement led to a new understanding within the medical profession of the experience of stillbirth, and of the development of new forms of support for mourning parents and families. The development in the 1950s and 1960s of a systemic model of psychotherapy, focusing on the interaction between children and parents and within families, has grown into the substantial body of theoretical knowledge and therapeutic techniques used in the Tavistock's training and research in family therapy.

The Understanding Your Child series has an important place in the history of the Tavistock Clinic. It has been issued in completely new form three times: in the 1960s, the 1990s, and in 2004. Each time the authors, drawing on their clinical background and specialist training, have set out to reflect on the extraordinary story of 'ordinary development' as it was observed and experienced at the time. Society changes, of course, and so has this series, as it attempts to make sense of everyday accounts of the ways in which a developing child interacts with his or her parents, carers and the wider world. But within this changing scene there has been something constant, and it is best described as a continuing enthusiasm for a view of development which recognizes the importance of the strong feelings and emotions experienced at each stage of development.

In many ways this volume initiates a new stage in the developmental process, just as *Understanding Your Baby* marked the beginning of the 'Understanding Your Child' series as a whole. It embarks boldly on such themes as independence, the testing of boundaries and the impact of physical and emotional change. Margot Waddell truly brings these issues to life through her thoughtful comments and use of illuminating examples. She is aware that these 'new' themes have a history themselves, and offers an approachable account of this period of transition when a strong independent impulse comes into conflict with earlier patterns of behaviour and a wish for security.

Jonathan Bradley
Child Psychotherapist
General Editor of the Understanding Your Child series

Introduction

Caught between lost childhood and unrealized adulthood, 12–14- year-olds often experience the most conflict-laden, bewildering and challenging years of all. These years may be quite as bewildering, as full of conflict and challenge to parents attempting to understand what is happening as they are to the young adolescents themselves – torn between both wanting, and not wanting, to be understood. This is a period of new kinds of friendship, of burgeoning sexuality, of changing interests and beginning awareness. It is a time of transition from a place in the family to a place in the outside world.

This process of transition, and the extraordinarily different forms it takes, can become all-consuming. It is a time of anxiety, apprehension and expectation, of the fear and thrill of the unknown. It is a time when, physically, growth is occurring more rapidly than at any other stage except in the womb and when, alongside that, changes in mental and emotional growth are at their most insistent and most demanding.

Boundaries are being tested, assumptions questioned, losses endured. The 12-year-old "child", newly out of junior or primary school, is struggling to relate the old world to the new, undergoing an intimidating and intoxicating rite of passage, clinging to the familiar, fascinated by the untried. By 14, the "young person" may seem to have abandoned childish things and to be precariously launched into a personal and social world of immense complexity, but as yet with no certainty, no clear goals nor firm direction. The central preoccupation is one of personal identity – "Who am I?"

The mother of a 12-year-old boy and a 14-year-old girl was heard to say to a friend with children of similar age: "I must get back to the kids. They seem to want me there even more now than when they were little. There's so much to say." "You're lucky your children still talk to you at all," was the reply. "I haven't the faintest idea what mine are up to or what they're thinking about. I find myself full of anxiety and just hoping for the best."

Most parents will recognize that the 12–14-year-olds, each in his or her own particular way, are going through dramatic changes and that the task of adapting to these changes is a turbulent one, for child and parent alike. Perhaps harder to recognize is the fact that change is involved for themselves as well. Many parents will have been developing with their child all along. At this age, however, it becomes evident that the understanding that is so crucial to the child's sense of security and self-esteem is based more firmly than ever in the parents' continuing ability to question what they thought they knew, to bear not knowing, to examine themselves, to learn from experience and perhaps especially, to tolerate rejection – be it in the form of withdrawal, negativity, abuse or duplicity – in the hope that this may temporarily be the painful path that separation takes. Being the parent of a 14-year-old will very likely feel quite different from being one of a 12-year-old – sometimes lonelier, sometimes richer, usually more difficult. Parents may discover new kinds of friendship as well as antagonism. Often they feel tested to the limit – "I love you but I don't always like you," is a not unfamiliar response.

How can all this be thought about, be understood? The thinking and the understanding may now be experienced as more problematic and more painful than ever before. This book explores the social, emotional and psychological tasks of 12–14-year-olds. It considers responses to the physical changes of puberty, to anxieties about sexuality, to problems of identity. It reflects on different kinds of friendship, especially those conducted in groups, and on the relationship between the changing demands of school and of family life. It looks at the ordinary expressions of desire, doubt and enthusiasm characteristic of the age group, and at the ways in which things may go wrong, the pitfalls, strains and worries for both children and parents that may get expressed in the many forms of self-harm characteristic of this age group: drugs, alcohol, cutting, eating disorders, delinquency. It thinks about the difficulty of maintaining a balance between the recognition and encouragement of greater freedom and the need for protection from the frightening possibilities which are suddenly opening up. Yet despite the multifold problems that assail child and parent alike, understanding what is likely to be going on for young people of this age may suggest ways in which parents may better enjoy, help and support them.

1

Other Bodies: Other Selves

Fourteen-year-olds tend to think about being 12 as belonging to a distant past, almost to a different person. These are typical reflections:

- "At 12 I expected to be looked after 24 hours of the day. I was treated like a child. Now I'm treated like a grown-up."
- "I was interested in being at home and in childish things, playing games like 'Had'. Now I'm interested in competitive sports and going out with friends, just anywhere."
- "I used to be good but now I do things to upset people – being bad-tempered, unreasonable, selfish, teasing and calling people unpleasant names."
- "I'm more interested in my friends now than in my family."
- "I didn't have many worries about boys. I do now and it takes over my work."
- "I was looked after then. Now I feel on my own."
- "At 12 I just lived in disguise, trying to survive. Now I can be more myself."
- "I moved from telling my parents everything to not telling them anything, even if it was completely unimportant."
- "When I was 12, to attract a girl maybe I would act hard and be very physical. Now I would talk to them and listen to what they have to say."
- "Family used to be so important, but suddenly I didn't want anything to do with them. In fact I wished they'd all die."

- "I certainly didn't want to be 12 for long. I wanted to be older, wearing a padded bra and traipsing around town trying to get into places."

- "I don't pine for my mum any more."

What is it that has happened between being the dependent child, whose emotional and creature needs were taken care of "24 hours a day", and being the young adolescent who is busy putting away "childish things" and who doesn't "pine for mum any more"?

While most parents of 12-year-olds will have no difficulty acknowledging, often wistfully, that their child seems to be quite different from how he or she was even a few months ago, they will find it much easier to describe *what* is happening than to have much sense of *why*.

- "She's suddenly taken to wearing baggy sweaters/body suits/dying her hair/wanting a nose stud."

- "He spends all his time in his room/in front of a mirror/on his mobile/reading magazines/playing computer games."

- "She's always starting rows about trivial things."

- "He won't wear the expensive jacket he was so desperate for only a few weeks ago."

The "children" may have as little idea as the parent about what is really going on. They find themselves feeling angrier, moodier, more anxious, more lonely, more excited, more frightened, not "themselves". Their responses to this strange state of affairs and the form these responses take in the family, at school, or in the outside world, will be thought about in later chapters. First, it is important to establish what really is going on at a basic, physical level, and then to look at the various ways in which young people try to adjust to what is happening to them.

Puberty: bodily changes

A child may well say, "What's happening to me?" Biological changes are taking place at this time over which he or she has no control. These are the physiological, anatomical, hormonal changes called "puberty". Puberty occurs in different bodies at different times, at different rates and in different ways. It usually happens earlier for girls than for boys. Some nine-year-old girls are already menstruating, some do not begin until they are 15 or 16. But for both boys and girls, the most usual time for puberty is between 12 and 14.

Each is becoming sexually, though not necessarily emotionally, an adult. The girls begin to have periods, to develop breasts and pubic hair. The shape and contours of their bodies are rapidly changing, often with a sudden increase in weight. They are sweating, smelling and often suffering unfamiliar aches and cramps. The boys experience their first ejaculations (usually initially in wet dreams). They often have a sudden increase in growth, they fill out, develop bodily hair, possibly spots, their voices change. They, too, sweat and smell. They become awkward and clumsy in their unfamiliar bodies.

These are the external characteristics. The processes of adjustment to such characteristics, emotionally and behaviourally, are what "adolescence" is. The responses to the external changes are seldom straightforward and they may be greeted with a wide variety of feelings – from denying they are happening at all, to confusion, to dread, to apprehension, to relief, to delight. Usually the feelings are mixed: pride and disgust, excitement and worry and, above all, self-consciousness.

Typical anxieties

Fathers often know little of these reactions. Mothers may know more about their daughters' worries than those of their sons. But, even so, the anxious question at bedtime about whether it's "normal to have one nipple bigger than the other", or "I've got a hard lump on one side and not the other – do you think it's cancer?" tends to represent the very tip of an iceberg that is laden with puzzles, confusions, anxieties, comparisons and mysteries.

Acquaintance with the so-called facts of life by this age does not mean that the young person in question really understands what is going on. Parents may feel that teachers, or preferably they themselves, have described to these young interrogators all that is necessary about sexual development, inter-course and reproduction. But such factual explanations tend to be a very different matter from the actual experience of the bodily changes and sexual feelings that are occurring in them as individuals. They are different, too, from the enormous variety of questions which arise in relation to the now most important and interesting person in the world, namely themselves.

- "Tracy says you can't go swimming if you have a period."
- "If you masturbate does it mean you can't have a baby?"
- "Susan says if the blood's brown to start with it means you'll be infertile."

These are some girls' remarks with which many mothers will be very familiar. The boys tend to be less open about things. But in each case, younger brothers and sisters tend suddenly to be chased out of the bathroom and the door locked. Requests are made for healthier food. Faddishness begins. Unexpected questions arise: "Is cereal good for you?", "Do crisps give you spots?" The reason for no longer wanting to go swimming eventually turns out not to be the chlorine, as stated, but the spotty back; or "Mum, none of the other boys are circumcised"; or "They've all got pubic hair except me". Occasionally such statements may be the rare and only indications of agonies in the showers, or the reason for unexpectedly not wanting to go to camp. "I'm not as tall as the others" will pop miserably out amidst what had seemed to be a problem with maths homework. Some boys will discuss with a parent why it is that an erect penis seems to shrink when in repose, but most will attempt, uncertainly, to glean such crucial information from other sources – films, books, the Net, gossip among friends of their own age, older boys.

Parents' responses

The sorts of comments just quoted represent an enormous range of conscious worries which parents may hear something of, and have to be ready to cope with and listen to as they arise. Yet it is usually important to be neither too probing nor too curious if the anxieties are not volunteered. A respectful, although not uninterested, distance is usually required, particularly with the boys, one which nonetheless conveys concern and a readiness to talk should the occasion arise.

Many young teenagers no longer feel that parents are the appropriate figures to turn to for answers to these new questions about the onset of puberty. The reasons are often quite disparaging: "They'd be too embarrassed", "They wouldn't know anyway". Or they may indicate vulnerability: "They might laugh at me". But the true sources of this distancing of parents from the young person's intimate life are complex, belonging to another level of feeling which underlies the more conscious ones just discussed. The hormonal and chemical changes which bring about physical growth and development at this time also reactivate passionate feelings and impulses, basically of love and hate, which were typical of the infant and very young child's relation to his or her parents. The commonly heard despairing cry of the 13-year-old's parents, "Oh stop being so infantile", is perhaps more accurate than is often realized.

The psychological changes of early adolescence revive a confusion of early longings towards, and aversions from, each parent, the intensity of which may be as baffling to the young person in question as it is disturbing to the adult. This intensity is related to the fact that there are now particular dangers attached to these passions, ones which make them especially hard to manage. For the sexually mature body of the young teenager has become technically able to *realize* the longings and *carry out* the aversions. The social necessity to begin separating from parent and family and to find a place in the social world is thus also fuelled by the much more primitive and unconscious necessity to let go of the parent, or parents, as figures to whom primary loving and hating feelings are directed and eventually to find substitutes for them in an intimate relationship outside the home.

For single-parent children or those whose parents have separated, the hormonally driven impulses and drives may pose particular problems, the necessary process of separation and detachment sometimes taking more violently rejecting forms than in two-parent families. This can be even more so if one or other parent is finding a new partner and adult sexuality is thus evident to the young, as will become clear in the following chapter.

2

Sexuality

For most, the physical changes of puberty mean that sexuality becomes an inescapable concern of central and compelling interest and importance. Although, in a sense, they have been sexual beings from the moment of their birth, 12–14-year-olds feel their sexuality to be like an entirely new, often dreadful, sometimes exciting experience. For it is sexual curiosity, sexual urges and sexual anxieties which most powerfully affect and fuel their relationships to themselves, their parents, friends and friendship groupings as never before. And it is often parents' complicated feelings about their own sexuality, both past and present, together with their understandable urges towards prohibitions, attaching to feared sexually transmitted infections and diseases or to teenage pregnancies, that can make it hard to adopt a helpful attitude towards their young adolescent.

There are some similarities in the boy's and the girl's sexual experience at this stage, but there are also some very important differences. Each, for example, is struggling to sort out their masculine and feminine sides. The struggle will certainly have been present in younger years, but with the arrival of puberty it becomes more pressing to resolve because of the need to establish sexual identity in relation to thinking about actual sexual partners and in relation to establishing a firm sense of gender. Both boys and girls are engaged with letting go the relationship with their parents as being central and special. But, at a more primitive level, they are again having to deal with the earliest relationship to their mothers. Feelings of blissful at-oneness and of savage rivalry are again stirred – sometimes expressed towards the mother herself and her relationship with her husband or partner, sometimes towards other figures, who in some way "stand for" the parental couple in the young person's unconscious phantasy.

Very early and often largely unconscious fears and phantasies[1] are reactivated at this time. They tend to find expression in dreams rather than in conscious thought, or in films which, in explicitly playing on such themes, are often of particular fascination to this age group. They also find expression in sudden bursts of unexpected and uncharacteristic behaviour – "acting out" as it is sometimes called – which may afterwards baffle and upset the young person quite as much as those others concerned.

The central anxiety for the boy is often that of being shut up inside a bad place, being stuck, trapped, losing his penis and/or his mind. The girl may have fears of invasion or occupation by something terrifying that will get inside and wreak havoc, in particular destroying her capacity to have babies. In that each sex also, to some extent, identifies with the other, versions of these fantasies may be shared. Such images, thoughts and anxieties are common and often stir the dramatic swings between passionate love and passionate hate which are so characteristic of this age group. One of the central conflicts tends to be that of how to reconcile these two very different sorts of impulse and feeling into a more integrated sense of self.

Masturbation

For many 12–14-year-olds, one source of relief from such tensions may be through masturbation – touching and finding sexual pleasure in parts of their own bodies, particularly their genitals. The guilt that this often engenders may be not so much about the masturbation itself as about the daydreams and fantasies that accompany it. For sexual thoughts at this age often have aggressive, lurid or perverse aspects to them which the young person finds unfamiliar and disturbing. A kind of mental experimentation goes on, fuelled by the recent hormonal changes, which may become a source of unspoken conflict, in that the experience is both alarming and gratifying at the same time.

---

1   "Phantasy" with a "ph" is a term used in psychoanalysis when describing the contents of the continuous inner unconscious mental life of a person. "Fantasy" with an "f" denotes the term for everyday, conscious imaginative life. Put more simply, phantasy denotes an unconscious process, fantasy a conscious one.

Masturbation usually disturbs parents too – who perhaps forget, or do not wish to remember, how they themselves felt at that age. The time when masturbation was prohibited has, on the whole, passed and there is now a more general recognition that beginning to masturbate is a quite normal aspect of adolescence. Yet parents may rightly find themselves concerned if they feel that masturbation has become a *substitute* for making any real contact with others – contact based in feelings of affection and love as well as lust and desire. When a young adolescent indulges in frequent masturbation but with no sign of any actual relationship, then some encouragement towards taking risks, or getting to know others as real people, rather than as fantasied figures, may be required. Really only the parents can know, almost by the "feel" of things, at what point to start worrying about, for example, their "child" seeming to be "wired up" to the net rather than "linked up" with others in any meaningful, emotional way. Similarly, only parents can know whether their particular child's interest in certain books, films, magazines, videos or websites is one that that child can take in his or her stride, or whether the interest is stirring impulses and sensations which may become hard to manage. It may be, for example, that feelings of sexual excitement have become attached to a range of quite unfamiliar urges and anxieties: perhaps to fears about abandonment, for example, about conflict, rejection, guilt, exclusion, recklessness, even cruelty. Seeking such excitement may be an expression of a difficulty of engaging with painful emotional areas that need to be recognized rather than avoided.

Unfortunately, parents are seldom in a position to know what exactly the young are exposing themselves to, or being exposed to by friends and older adolescents. There may be quite justified disquiet about what is being downloaded in the early hours of the morning, or about what, exactly, is being engaged with in the "chat rooms". The hazards, as well as the advantages, of new technology are keenly felt by parents of this age group.

Perhaps, however, despite misgivings, it needs to be borne in mind that the common teenage interest in what might seem to parents excessively explicit, or even perverse, areas of sexuality may have positive aspects too, to be understood rather than condemned. For young adolescents, like everyone else, have perverse thoughts and interests, and also a degree of voyeuristic curiosity. It can be a relief to them to discover that such preoccupations are commonly shared and expressed by others too. It may also be reassuring to have an opportunity to "rehearse" their fantasies about, for example, lovemaking by watching it on screen, or reading about it in teen magazines, before they come anywhere near actually doing anything about it themselves. Looking back to being this age, many young people, especially girls, comment that their unquenchable appetite for sexual information was a lot more to do with self-education than with activity. The titillating explicitness of the pre-teen and early-teen magazines often has quite as much to do with shared girliness and helpful instructions as with any actual behaviour, although there will always be a few girls regarded as being "hardcore". As one 15-year-old put it, "We were all trying to get off with as many people as possible, but it didn't amount to much more than kissing, really."

Over-protectiveness and denial on a parent's part may make it harder for a young person to experiment in fantasy, and to some extent in fact, with these exciting, frightening and often contradictory feelings. To take no responsibility at all, however, may be to allow the young an excess of over-stimulating or arousing experiences – especially those involving violence or degradation – which can stir up considerable guilt as well as erotic excitement. It is a very rare adolescent who is able to talk to parents about such things in any detail. Fathers can sometimes try to share with sons an attempt at smutty humour but this is usually felt to be intrusive and embarrassing. Mothers may get a bit further in discussing the emotional aspects of sexual experiences. But for the most part this is an area which, it should be assumed, is little shared though very preoccupying, and significantly contributes to mood swings, bouts of unexpected anger, elation or withdrawal. It is hard for parents to be attentive while being neither probing nor prohibiting; to be available without sitting in judgement.

Technically knowing the facts of life in no sense lessens the intense curiosity about all aspects of sexuality, especially that of the adult world. Both boys and girls will be very taken up with adult sexuality, their investigations and imagination usually being directed not so much towards their own parents as towards, for example, the private lives of teachers, or of older siblings. The idea of parents having an ongoing sexual relationship at all is seldom a welcome one. In conversation with her 13-year-old group of friends, Laura stated that she was *convinced* that her parents hadn't "done it" since she was herself conceived. "Nor have mine," agreed some of the others. "But what about your little sister?" a friend asked. "Well maybe once," Laura replied. She was absolutely shattered a few weeks later when her parents told her that they had decided to have a last baby. Apart from the understandable jealousy towards a younger rival, Laura was uncomfortably confronted with the fact of adult sexuality, not in general – which was a daily preoccupation for herself and her friends – but in the particularly galling case of her own parents.

What can easily be underestimated is the loss that goes with the necessary displacing of parents from their central position in the child's inner and outer world. Some degree of self-esteem is bound to be linked to the high regard in which they have held their parents hitherto, and also to the high regard that they, in turn, have often enjoyed from their parents as well. When, as so commonly at this age, that regard becomes significantly diminished, there may be quite a dramatic drop in the sense of self-worth – one of the many sources of feelings of emptiness or void which so many adolescents describe. While seemingly wilfully inviting criticism and judgement, there often remains a covert craving for admiration and respect. The apparent contradiction was well expressed by a 13-year-old, Meg: eyeing her tattoo and belly-button stud she wistfully commented on how much she wanted to achieve something that her mum "would reckon".

With one set of ties being loosened and another not yet made, there is a period of transition in which self-preoccupation often predominates. Whether it is putting the self down or building it up, the adolescent "self" tends to be of supreme interest. One teacher in an all-boys school described the distinctive "swagger" of the "little 12-year-olds", constantly pushing against the year above and adopting sexually explicit language as a common vocabulary of abuse.

Making new relationships

It is at this point that the differences between the two sexes have to be emphasized as well. First, the girl's eventual full sexual partner is very likely to be from the opposite sex to her mother, the boy's from the same sex. Second, in terms of his anatomy and physical experiences, the boy will be much clearer about sexual desire, how it feels and how it is expressed, than the girl at this same age. And third, there are important cultural factors which have a major impact on each, in terms of what is expected of a girl and of femininity, and what of a boy and of masculinity.

For the girl, as the tie to the mother loosens, the need is very strong for intense friendship with other girls. There is a tendency to idealize and often to sexualize older girls or young women who can replace what is being let go. There is a tendency, too, to be drawn to more powerful or more attractive girls whose dominant characters lend status to their views and activities.

But one has to bear in mind that the mother was the source not only of love, but also of rage and frustration – feelings which now often get expressed about, and towards, girlfriends. If the relationship with her mother has been generally good, a girl can more easily feel, particularly when her periods begin, that she can begin to relinquish her little-girl dependency on her mother and be like her in a more grown-up and feminine way. Many mothers, however, are upset to encounter what they feel to be their daughter's unexpected negativism at this stage. This kind of hostile and often contemptuous rejection can occur with particular ferocity when the relationship in the past has not been easy and the young adolescent now finds herself both seeking, and fighting, a much earlier childlike attachment. She wants, in other words, to cling onto something from the past which she feels she still needs – perhaps from a sense that she had never got enough – but also finds herself feeling angry and resentful about that clingy neediness and pulling away again with unpredictable suddenness and savagery. Many mothers find themselves deeply shaken by the verbal, and even physical, abuse they may be subjected to when their hitherto loving little girl turns into a harridan for no apparent reason.

The complexity of the changing relationship with their mother contributes to a greater tendency for girls to become intensely, though often ambivalently, emotionally entangled with other girls – more so than does a boy with his peer group. This struggle is evident in the painful reality of just how nasty girls of this age can be to one another, how cliquish and preoccupied they are with the daily dramas of treachery and betrayal, how subtle and universal is the experience of bullying and being bullied. Much is required of such friends: sameness, resilience, loyalty, often exclusivity; partnership in secrets, possibly with a sexual content of a sort which heightens the excitement and the erotic flavour; the sharing of fantasies, usually about boys or imagined adult sexual relationships. All this is reassuring. It makes for a sense of "normality". The girls find in each other qualities which either confirm what they are like themselves or express what they would like to be like. The relationships the girl has with other girls, with teachers and perhaps, in fantasy, with models or singers and so on, have elements of the original bond with mother, but they exist at a safer distance.

The nature and significance of early adolescent groupings will be further explored in Chapter 4, but in the present context, a link needs to be established between the characteristic love/hate relationship with the mother and the intensely sexual interest that can get whipped up among the girls as they struggle with their central preoccupation of defining themselves as different from their mothers.

On the whole, then, the inner world of the pubescent girl is predominantly peopled by other females. It is an intensely sexual time: boys are exciting, fascinating, contemptible, sometimes to be "gone out with" or "snogged", but primarily to be talked about, thought about and fantasized about with the other girls. There are endless whispered conversations about who's "doing it", about what "it" might feel like, and about what sexual desire really *is*. Describing herself at 14, Clare (now 18) expressed the state of mind very clearly:

> I felt totally miserable, either furious or self-hating all the time. Writing a diary was a bit of a help, but what finally made the difference was finding Emily. We just did everything together. We told each other our secrets, our fantasies, our worst fears, things that we'd never tell anybody else. We went everywhere together; we slept in the same bed together. I'm sure I was kind of in love with her, but it didn't seem sexual. She made all the difference to my world. Sometimes I even thought for a moment that I might really be beautiful like her, it was just that I didn't look it. We were part of a group of friends which were really important too, but the close relationship was always with our best friends – for me, Emily.

Clare's experience was not primarily sexual, as she says. But there were probably sexual elements in it nonetheless. Commonly there is an intense wish, for example, to touch breasts as comparisons are being conducted for relative growth and size. Girls often dream about other girls; experience first being "in love" in relation to girls; become fascinated with finding out about lesbian relationships and, not infrequently, "faking" *being* lesbian – a distinctively "cool" phenomenon in some friendship groups.

For boys, sex tends to be less mysterious. Having had erections from a young age, they are in no doubt at all what sexual desire is, nor where it is located. Their groups are also close and similar to the girls' in the sense that they tend to be made up of boys like themselves. Again similarities are reassuring when being different is so terrifying. The anxieties for the boys tend to be different. Potency and performance may be centrally important issues for some; for others, risking an advance into the apparently unassailably superior world of the girls seems unthinkable; for yet others fears of being castrated by their sophisticated girl peers can push them into the safety in numbers of the all-boy group.

On another level, the loss of a sense of identity that goes with the letting go of the world of childhood and the strong bond with mother, is a bit reduced when a boy is surrounded by others who, in the all-boy group, are in his own image. With him, however, this loss of mother is also partly to do with having to relinquish what might have been regarded, hitherto, as a quite feminine aspect of his personality, one which he now feels he has to let drop, along with his mother, if he is to be confident among the older boys. The result is often the kind of exaggeration of male attributes which is especially clear in groups and is often modelled on quite crude notions, even caricatures, of manhood – the kind of male "swagger" described by the boys' teacher makes its appearance, frequently accompanied by an altered accent, and, as one 12-year-old put it, even a change "in how low you wear your trousers".

Homosexuality

The kind of exaggerated male characteristics just described may, however, also be an expression of the anxiety, so typical of this age and particularly among the boys, about being homosexual. Most boys, and many girls, will, in the course of sorting out their confused desires and urges, have homosexual feelings and may, not uncommonly, experiment with homosexual relationships. Such experiments are often an important part of establishing sexual preference as a basic component of their sense of who they are. Although in relation to prevailing cultural norms, they may cause fear, guilt, distress or bravado, these kinds of experimentation should certainly be regarded as part of the ordinary process of growing up. The degree to which homosexuality is felt to be upsetting, or not, is strongly related to family and cultural attitudes, but the anxiety in the adolescents themselves about something as basic as to which gender they feel they are attracted should not be underestimated.

A rather clear, albeit extreme, example of this phenomenon is the experience of 14-year-old John, who had been very close to his dad until his parents' marriage broke up when he was about 12. As the eldest in the family, he had become very supportive of his mother, who had four other younger children to look after. Soon after John's fourteenth birthday his teacher became worried about his missing so much school. She discovered from his mother that he had become quite uncharacteristically rude, rejecting and angry towards her and totally preoccupied with anxiety about being homosexual. It emerged that he had also become very worried about whether or not he had actually turned off the appliances in the house – especially taps – and whether he had shut the door securely.

In the course of some sessions with the school counsellor, John came to realize that although he hated the idea of being homosexual, it was less frightening than experiencing physical desire towards his mother. He had first become aware of this desire in a surge of jealous rage when he saw a waiter flirtatiously touch his mother's bottom soon after his father had left home. His anger with his mother was a painful attempt to distance her from his passionate feelings, and to make her undesirable in his mind by rubbishing her. Possibly his worry about turning things off was an expression of his fear of not being in control of his feelings generally, and, perhaps more specifically, of his ejaculations.

Having understood some of this, John was able to direct his feelings towards a more appropriate person – a girl of his own age to whom he became attracted soon after his counselling sessions ended. The other worries became much more manageable. In this case John's dad was not physically there to assert marital rights which might have inhibited his son's incestuous anxieties. Nor was he able to offer any emotional support to John because of John's fury and disillusionment with his father for, as John saw it, abandoning the family home. John felt his dad was a failure and regarded him as an object of contempt. His criticisms, only to some extent justifiable, were fuelled by primitive feelings of anger, fear and hatred. His parents' marital difficulties had made the ordinary problems of sorting out his respective relationships to them a lot harder for, like everyone else, he had had, in his infancy, painfully to acknowledge his father's supremacy and to take his place in relation not to his mother alone, which was what he desired, but to his parents as a couple. Having his mother again to himself had stirred up early guilt and anxieties which he found confusing and unmanageable.

Jack vividly remembered his discovery of prejudice in relation to homosexuality in his own age group and how he was supported in sorting out his feelings by an understanding mother. He described the social difficulties he ran into when he started "making friends" at 14, instead of just "being close to the lads" in the school football team and Sunday league matches, associations which, as he said, had nothing to do with intimacy.

> At 14 I started "making friends" with girls instead of just "going out with them". I also made friends with quite an effeminate boy whom everyone thought was homosexual. But he was, in fact, much more

interesting than everyone else. Blokes are often cruel at that age about difference. They stopped talking to me because I was a homosexual's friend. It would have been much easier for me not to be friends with this bloke and I got very upset about it. Luckily, my mum was great. She said, "You must keep him as your friend, despite what others say." My mum was a big influence on me. I suppose she was always sort of overseeing things, but never overlooking them.

John and Jack's painful experiences will each, in their different ways, have been ones from which much could be learned about themselves and the world. More superficially, at a time of such frantic need for attention and of fear of being left on the margins, or disregarded as "nerdy" or "nondescript", experimenting with a homosexual identity can be a way of seeming special or different. Linda described how, at her all-girls school, it was considered quite daring to be lesbian, but dismissed any such claim on actual sexual identity at 13 or 14 as more to do with image than with the sort of genuine identification that might become established a bit later on. Similarly, some boys, despite the generally homophobic atmosphere that prevails in this age group, might "camp it up" – again gaining a reputation for a sort of extravagance and distinctiveness.

Most parents know little of the difficulties of these endless sexual negotiations, for deeper worries about homosexuality tend to remain very private. There may be clues to the worries in a particular readiness to use homosexual epithets as forms of abuse, perhaps signifying an anxiety about gender orientation which is swiftly, cruelly and defensively attributed elsewhere in a "let it be him, or her, and not me" mode. Such defensiveness, however, may also be related to many young people's conviction that were their parents to know, or suspect, that they were gay those parents would, by turn, be horrified/furious/devastated/rejecting and so on. It is this conviction, so often misplaced, that can seriously increase anxiety and a sense of loneliness, leading to much unnecessary pain and concealment. Parents do need to be ready to enable their children to be most honestly who they feel themselves to be, however different that may turn out to be from themselves.

Old emotions, new feelings

The physical changes of puberty arouse feelings which are powerful, new and therefore mysterious and alarming. Where sexuality is concerned, they are alarming because they belong to areas of the unconscious, rooted in very early experience and therefore not available to be thought about in any ordinary way. This hiddenness may offer some partial explanation for the sense, so common at this age, of guilt and shame about something which remains, somehow, unidentifiable and nameless; 12–14-year-olds do not know what they are so ashamed about, or guilty of. There is no specific answer because that answer is likely to lie in these unknown areas of desire and rage.

The small child's anxieties that whatever has gone wrong is basically his or her own fault and also that thinking something might be the same as doing it, are often revived and intensified by early adolescent sexual and aggressive impulses. Looking back on these years, one 19-year-old, Joanna, put it very well:

> It was all very frightening. I thought, "I'm going crazy" and "It's all my fault". "No," I thought, "it's not my fault, it's all my dad's fault." "Whichever way it is, it's terrible." I felt completely misunderstood all the time – either furious or self-hating, scared of what was going to happen. Would it be like this for the rest of my life? I denied what was happening to my body and at the same time agonized about whether there was something wrong in finding people sexy.

Joanna had concerned and loving parents who would have regarded them-selves as understanding and emotionally in touch. But they were also begin-ning to experience something that will be familiar to many parents: that the models that they felt they could offer no longer seemed relevant or helpful to their children.

What is often being sought in the various types of grouping and stormy behaviour at this age is some alternative source of identification from the sexual stereotypes which their parents are usually taken to represent. The girls may be struggling to find a positive identification which is neither only maternal nor merely sexy. For boys, common male stereotypes may seem not only compelling and erotic, but also at odds with their own more tender and caring feelings. Whether in the case of boys or girls, one may be fairly certain, in the area of sexuality in particular, that between 12 and 14 there are intense pressures coming from outside and inside simultaneously. Many of them describe the immense strain of "never feeling you can really be yourself"; of "being pulled and pushed in all directions"; of "having to be in disguise"; of "living in a kind of virtual reality, where no one really knows you, even yourself, and you feel lonely and desperate most of the time".

Being aware of this kind of stress and yet excluded from it is usually very hard for parents to bear. The best that can be done may simply be for them to realize how momentous a struggle may be going on and to support and respect that struggle, in so far as they can.

3

School Life
The Primary/Secondary Divide

Most children between the ages of 12 and 14 find themselves much more drawn to their friends than to their family. They are making the transition, at some point during these years, from a known and familiar way of life to a new and strange one: from primary to secondary school, from junior or middle to senior school. In general, parents find that they have very much less to do with school life on a day-to-day basis than previously – perhaps especially if they were used to meeting children in the playground, going into school with them, and chatting to teachers. Now they feel almost left out: they don't have a "sense" of the school or of the nature of their children's daily experiences any more.

For parents, teachers now tend to have names but not faces: the new rules, visible and invisible, are confusing; they are no longer familiar with particular and likely sources of anxiety in their child. They may be aware that their 12-year-old is under strain, but do not know its source nor how to help. More importantly, they are often no longer accorded a position in which they can be of significant help. For the junior/senior, primary/secondary divide is much bigger than many anticipate. This unexpected sense of impotence is almost always very testing for parents, and for mothers, in particular, who often find the degree of exclusion so "unbearable" that they may resort to unwonted intrusiveness. One mother described her pain at being shut out as follows:

> I never thought I would stoop to this, but I did start reading Katie's diary and was horrified by what I learned. I had no idea what she was up to. When she discovered what I was doing there was an almighty row and she screamed that she hated me and would never trust me again.

What this mother learned was how distressed and confused her daughter was. Katie was sleeping with a much older boy who she felt was "just using her", and was frequently cutting her arms and thighs to get some relief from a sense of unbearable, unspeakable, and therefore unshareable, tension.

Fortunately for Katie, her mother's response was supportive rather than punitive and there was eventually even an admission that the diary's being left in plain sight was no accident. Katie was desperate for help, but the fact that the very figure she needed was the one she was busy rejecting had cut her off from her previous source of support and comfort. This boundary, between intrusiveness and neglect, is one of the most tormenting for many parents. Turning a blind eye can result in young adolescents going beyond what they can quite manage, whatever they think themselves capable of at the time. Yet however hard the young may resist, challenge and cajole, establishing firm, yet reasonable, parental boundaries is often reassuring to them, though there is seldom agreement as to where the lines should actually be drawn.

The change of school is often eagerly looked forward to. Many children have had enough of their old school by the time they reach the top, but for a large number the shock of entering "big school", and the unexpectedly different way of life that it involves, takes a long time to adjust to – often the whole of the first year. As one 12-year-old put it, "It's awful. You have to hide everything and change the way you talk, how you act and even how you walk." Many comment on how the sheer size of the school can feel overwhelming at first; being among the smallest in such a huge institution is very threatening and scary. It is not easy for parents to take in just what an impact this transition has; that this really *is* a rite of passage, one that demands survival skills, inner strength and degrees of resilience which may now be being tested as never before. The comments at the beginning of Chapter 1 about wanting, at 12, "to be looked after 24 hours of the day" have now to be considered in relation to how little looking-after the 12-year-olds feel they receive at school. Some find it very difficult to adjust, for example, to getting to school and back on their own; to having a different teacher for each subject; dealing with expectations that they will take responsibility for communications within school and between home and school; and with assumptions that they will organize their homework properly. Even an apparently small change, like occupying a different classroom for different subjects, may open up a huge area of unexpected stress. In many schools, not only do all belongings constantly have to be carried from one place to another, but also the route between the two may offer extensive opportunities for pushing, shoving, casual bullying and humiliation of all kinds.

At this stage, the significance of relative body size and degree of physical and emotional development can hardly be exaggerated. Even such matters as precise age become of enormous significance. At a time when, for boys, physical prowess is everything, there is a world of difference between having a July birthday or a September birthday. This notional "year", denoting whether you are among the oldest or the youngest in the class, is felt to have a huge impact, on sexual confidence in particular. Popularity, being good at sport and able to fight are indissolubly linked. Jamie, a 17-year-old with a July birthday, spoke movingly of what he felt had disadvantaged him so badly in his first year at secondary school.

> You have to be big and strong to survive. Intelligence doesn't matter, you just have to be tall. Most of the girls go for older boys anyway, but if you're small, like me, you just hope you don't get bullied too badly at school and find ways of staying at home as much as you can.

Jamie's mother had become aware of her son's suffering only when she noticed that, unlike her daughter at the same age, Jamie was keeping to his room, watching sport and compulsively playing computer games, sometimes with a friend, usually alone. Checking with other boys' parents, she found that the retreat into television and computers was a common phenomenon among many of Jamie's peers, especially those who were a bit younger or less well developed physically. Jamie had experienced extensive bullying as a result of his being small and skinny and felt that the humiliation had had long-term consequences. Reflecting on boys' general experiences, he later said:

> Unless they feel they're the top man, in all the street gear and being fancied, boys can have a really bad time. They carry a lot at that age in private. School's a microcosm of society, really, guys being pseudo-strong and emotionally repressed. But when you're born has an awful lot to do with it.

The significance of precise age often has a different kind of meaning for girls. The more mature, the more likely it is that they will know older girls and be having relationships with older boys earlier than others in their year. The sexually active 13-year-old may well be among the oldest in her class, already looking more grown-up and confident, and attracting to herself girls who may, like her, be contemptuous of the insecurity of the boys of their own age.

These girls often regard themselves as much more knowing and better at reading and understanding emotional situations, which they do almost exclusively with their girlfriends. The resulting sexual confidence and activity may have much more to do with status than with any genuine sexual or loving feelings. Position in the pecking order tends to take precedence over more sincere or mature emotional encounters.

Making friends

All these considerations have a significant part in the general social stress of making friends, of dealing with the pain and pleasure of being excluded or included, unpopular or popular. Having never particularly noticed or cared about differences of race, class or gender before, for the 12-year-old such factors suddenly begin to divide up the school community into factions, hierarchies and cliques. In comprehensive schools, for example, racial groupings and the particular styles that attach to them, in terms of fashion, vocabulary, music, interests and attitudes, become much more obvious. Differences in family income also become more noticeable – enabling some to "do the clubs" and leaving others, of necessity, hanging around in parks or on street corners, or simply staying at home. With such differences, bullying, petty crime, mugging and theft often begin, organized around particular groupings, or rather around particular "gangings".

In short, 12-year-olds feel thrown in at the deep end to discover who they are in relation to how other children respond to them. Few children have spent their early school years with no experience of bullying, but entry into secondary school, partly *because* it is so stressful for everyone, tends to sharpen children's responses to feelings of uncertainty and difference. Looking back from the comparative safety of 19, Jane described those early days:

> I hated it really. It was such a burden looking confident when I didn't feel like that inside at all. Everyone was watching everyone *all* the time. I was aware of what I looked like practically every minute of the day. I always felt a complete outsider – not middle class enough for one group, not working class enough for the other, the wrong sex, the wrong race, the wrong colour. It all felt terrible. Most of all, I suppose, I discovered just how cruel girls can be to other girls – nasty, in subtle, undermining sorts of ways that left me feeling miserable with no one to talk to about it.

Parents' attitude to school

All this is not to say that some children don't take to secondary school like ducks to water. But it is perhaps more usual, in this first year, for children to suffer in ways that their parents may have a general sense of, but with little idea of the detailed experiences. Sometimes they discover this indirectly, when, for example, their child mysteriously develops tummy aches or head-aches and refuses to go to school, or is found to have been "bunking off". It is hard for a parent to recognize that something may lie behind these "illnesses" and "absences" and to have to face not being able to "make it better", as they might have been able to do in the past. Their son or daughter now has to manage largely alone. Yet struggling mainly without parents' help – if not without their support – though painful, may for young adolescents also be an important way of finding a place in the world and sorting out who they are, by way of developing new strengths, resilience and independence.

Despite feeling that their interest in school activities is no longer welcome, parents' attitudes to school life and teachers, in fact, remains very significant. Underneath the superficial casualness, the 14-year-olds usually *do* want parents to remember the name of the English teacher they have had for two years; to know roughly what is meant by the current slang; to recognize the sources of provocation and difficulty in their particular school – no lavatory paper, water turned off for most of the day, etc. Most of all, they need an interest to be taken in their achievements rather than in their failings. Sam, aged 13, whose father didn't live in the family any more, was always extremely anxious about his dad's good opinion of him. With anticipated pleasure, he took his excellent report round to show his father. "That's good, but why did you only get a C in French?" His father was never shown a report again.

It is usually helpful for a child to feel that parents are basically sympathetic to the school despite its inevitable deficiencies, and are also, generally, on the side of the teachers. Parents have to maintain a difficult balance between neither totally handing over responsibility for their child to the school nor, in turn, undermining the school's authority. This may at times be hard, especially in the light of the dramatic stories about teachers' behaviour and attitudes that can be recounted by the youngster with considerable relish. Simply siding with either party is seldom a good solution. For example, not to question an authoritarian school regime may seem to reinforce intolerant atti-tudes at home, leaving the child with nowhere to turn. Indeed it may lead to the child reproducing that same intolerance in his or her own group of friends, or, more likely, in relation to younger children. On the other hand, accepting the child's point of view at face value may not be helpful either. For at this age everything is likely to be exaggerated or polarized, being seen in extremes of good and bad and, above all, to be highly changeable.

In spite of this caveat, it is also very important for children of this age to feel that their views, say, of a teacher's unjust behaviour, are being taken seriously, neither written off as "that's life" nor made into a federal offence. Many 12–14-year-olds have an admirably fierce, though perhaps crude, sense of justice and some encouragement to see things tolerantly, or at least imaginatively from different angles is always helpful. If glaring injustices continue to be complained about over a period of time, then action may be required. There is always a fine line between parental interference and the abdication of concern and responsibility. Nonetheless, it is hard to get it right. Do you reprimand a child who is persecuting your daughter? Do you ring up her parents? Do you tell your daughter to stick it out? Or do you go to the school to complain? Resistant though they may seem to be, most children are reassured to feel that parents and school are cooperating. They also need to feel that their parents, whether still together or not, are basically in agreement over their schooling, along with their general welfare.

Thirteen-year-old Danny vividly described his pride and horror when his mum stormed into the headmaster's office to complain about his being victimized. Despite resistance and embarrassment, there may be great relief when a firm line is taken, particularly if the school's response is swift and appropriate. It requires careful judgement to decide when a child's complaint about being teased or badly treated at school is something the child should be encouraged to stand up to, and when it is a matter of being singled out and picked on to an unacceptable and cruel degree. Such a distinction usually requires sensitivity, over a period of time, to that particular child's moods and behaviour – whether there is a sense of depression, a reluctance to go to school, sleeplessness, deterioration in work, and so on. This vigilance, combined with discussion with the class teacher or staff concerned, may help to sort out how serious the problem is and whether one child has become the butt of particularly unkind attention.

Jasmine's parents noticed that for several weeks she had been sleeping badly, was prone to tears and unusually reluctant to go to school. To their gentle enquiries, she maintained, for some time, that nothing was wrong and would they please leave her alone. But late one night, she described to her mother her intense distress about the boys in her class picking on her and calling her names of a particularly crude, racist kind. She had also received some vicious, and unattributable, text and mobile phone messages – an especially cruel and increasingly common type of bullying in this age group. Jasmine swore her mother to secrecy – she would die rather than have it known that she was troubled by this and feared that telling someone would make it all worse.

The distress continued, however, and her mother, having discussed it with a couple of other parents, decided to mention her concern to the Year Head. His response was to air the issue with the whole class, not in relation to Jasmine's individual experience but as a matter of great concern to the school as a whole. Any more signs of such behaviour would, in future, be very firmly dealt with. Jasmine was immensely relieved that her parents and the school had cooperated without betraying her confidence, with the result that she herself had had to take neither the responsibility nor the blame.

It may, on the other hand, be the teacher who alerts the parents to problems a child is having with others in, or outside, the classroom. Teachers are in a special position to observe relations among these young teenagers and have immediate access to the many aspects of their lives which are now becoming less available to parents. Indeed teachers, during these years, may often have a very central role in a child's life. The capacity, on their part, to be receptive to the complex forms that a child's communications may take, and to understand and respond to those communications for what they really are, rather than what they may appear to be on the surface, can have an enormous impact on the individual child's school experience. For many children, the role of the teacher is of vital importance, the role of someone who is outside the immediate family, but yet has extensive experience of their behaviour and social relations, as well as their cognitive skills and intellectual development. In significant ways, then, teachers can function, for this age group, as parent substitutes, mediating the relationships between peer group and the adult world. Many young people attest to the significance for them of a teacher's interest and respect, and to the disastrous consequences of feeling disliked or discriminated against.

Any distinctive change in a young person's attitude or behaviour may be the first signal, to a sufficiently sensitive teacher, of some sort of anxiety, possibly needing to be addressed with the individual child and, if appropriate, with the family as well. Such a teacher may also be aware of the stresses and conflicts which often underlie so-called "attitude" and behaviour problems generally. The feeling of being understood rather than punished or disciplined may then support stronger and more hopeful development rather than fearfulness, despondency or further rebellion.

At 14, Nick was caught smoking cannabis with a group of friends. Not only had this taken place in the school grounds, but also it happened in a particular spot that was in full view of the staff room. Nick was very severely reprimanded, his parents were sent for and he was suspended from school for a week. His father realized that this uncharacteristically delinquent behaviour could be linked to the fact that Nick had been mugged earlier in the week by some older boys. His watch and trainers had been taken and he had been left severely shocked.

The school made no acknowledgement that there could be any connection between breaking rules and this kind of traumatic experience. Nick – though appreciating his father's understanding – became increasingly disaffected and difficult at school and his work temporarily suffered quite badly. Had a teacher been more sympathetic, at the time, to his particular predicament and offered a less rule-bound response, Nick's school life might have been a lot less disrupted.

The role of learning

There is a potentially huge expansion occurring at this stage in the range of ways of thinking and learning, of gathering information and acquiring technical skills. Because this expansion comes at the very time when so many other aspects of life are in flux, school activities often become an important barometer for how other things are going, and later exam results an indication of how things have been going. While there is no clear correlation between work difficulties and emotional difficulties, the ongoing general disparity, during adolescence, between the boys' and the girls' exam achievements do, nevertheless, attest to this phase of development, at least in contemporary culture, being especially challenging and difficult for the boys whose routes to maturity are felt to be so complex and fraught. There can, however, particularly among the girls, be an inverse relationship between intensity of commitment to studying and psychological well-being, for a tendency to overwork and a striving for perfection may indicate an excessive need for control through achievement as a way of defending against the more troubling aspects of the adolescent process itself.

Although many older adolescents will assert that they have no recollection of school work figuring at all between the ages of 12 and 14, it does seem that, in the midst of the general turmoil, some learning does still go on. The intellectual growth that can occur at this time has an important part to play in these young people's sense of themselves and their place in the world; in the discovery of new abilities and interests and in the promotion of self-esteem. Learning may also often function as another basis for relating to peers, although that aspect of things would, perhaps, seldom be admitted. Looking back to this time, 17-year-old Jonathan commented:

> The general line was always to complain about work, and make out that you weren't doing any. Although kids moan about school, you do learn and become interested, given the right teacher. School actually becomes a place you want to be and home can be a bit annoying and boring. Though few would admit to it, they are often thinking "Actually this is something I wouldn't mind learning about." They don't speak about it because being enthusiastic or clever isn't really on. But they do think, "This is basically OK."

Parents might be surprised to hear older teenagers agreeing with Jonathan's remark. In retrospect, most of his friends wished that their school had had a tighter grip on them and had offered more encouragement to keep working at the early stages. They felt that their friends had tended to take over in not altogether welcome ways and that work suffered, adding to the strains of the exams to come. This would not have been a view that many would have volunteered at the time, although some remembered becoming disaffected because they were bored or not sufficiently stretched. For these few, feeling fed-up and alienated seemed to be related to frustrations in learning and "getting on", and to too much attention having to be given to maintaining discipline rather than to the teaching itself.

For some, the new kind of work pressures of this age have their stressful side, stirring up competitiveness. For others, fears of failure or being driven towards excessive performance, in that these are likely also to be expressions of other kinds of problems, may feel quite unmanageable at times. For yet others, that same pressure may be enabling, encouraging awareness of new capacities and strengths and opening up unexpected worlds of interest and curiosity which support their developing personalities. It is, indeed, difficult for parents neither to alienate their children by over-protection, nagging and worry, nor to let them down or put them at risk by neglect or lack of interest. School now tends to seem a world apart, but parental involvement, encouragement and interest may still be much more important than is apparent. The stresses of group life are immense and may well spill over in disruptive ways into the family. In many households, the flashpoint is homework. Worried about their young adolescent's immersion in group life, fearful for his or her academic future, frustrated by what is felt to be the squandering of potential, and excluded from so many of their activities, parents often latch onto the doing or not-doing of homework with particular vigour.

It can be hard, both for the parent and the young person, to determine the real source of these understandable anxieties, and tempers tend to flare on both sides. Is the parent, in fact, in touch with, and expressing a version of, the child's own anxiety? Does the impetus come from parental competitiveness and ambition and not from what really matters to their son or daughter? The concerned parent is usually well aware that his or her attitude runs counter to the prevailing teenage culture and yet has to remain committed to trying to retain some kind of authority in the face of resentment, anger or sullen opposition.

However, in the young person's view, encouragement tends to be felt as censoriousness and support as unwelcome and intrusive. Taxing as these "set-to's" may be, perhaps it is helpful to bear in mind that these, too, are part of the separation process, part of the young person's struggle towards finding his or her own bases for deciding what matters and what is important, while simultaneously repudiating any such responsibilities, especially as represented by parental attitudes.

A sympathetic awareness of the nature of the struggles and the energy to go on trying and not to give up may, as always, play a crucial part in the young people's ability to get through them, whatever the intensity of opposition at the time.

4

Groups
Inclusion and Exclusion

Many teachers, parents and even older adolescents regard the ages of 12 to 14 as psychologically the most testing of all, both for the young people themselves and for those responsible for them. Now, it is not so much the "terrible twos" that stir parental anxiety, but the "terrible teens". Many adults will readily recognize and share bemusing descriptions of a restless group constantly on the move; a group who are rude and abusive, among whom there is a characteristic absence of attention span, concentration, thoughtfulness or respect; a group in which there may be an excessive show of confidence and cockiness, with little to substantiate it; one claiming rights and privileges but averse to responsibilities; one which represents itself as a clan of sorts, adopting the culture of young libertines: binge-drinking, flouting boundaries, smoking, drug-taking, bonding through music and fashion; one that is psychologically and behaviourally nigh out of control.

Many 13- or 14-year-old girls, erstwhile shy of their just-changing bodies, are now, according to these teachers and parents, proud and provocative, forming girl-gangs which tend to be more powerful, generally more cliquish and condescending than the less mature boys, and also more covert, subtle and deadly in their dominating behaviour and bullying techniques. The boys may express their need for mutual support and bonding in rather different ways. Almost in retreat, some may find kudos in appearing exaggeratedly streetwise, or, especially, through developing prowess in sport. In the absence of such immediate options, others turn, in increasing numbers, to alcohol and/or to drugs, or, in some cases, establish an early, intense, one-to-one relationship – a pseudo-marriage, as some scathing, but perhaps also envious, peers might describe it. The serious drug problems of mid- and late-adolescent young men tend to start in these early years, when finding and occupying a male role with any pride or confidence is felt to be so intimidating and often quite hopeless. Yet such underlying intimidation and hopelessness may, in turn, simply intensify what amount to the pseudo-solutions of substance abuse, self-harm, delinquency or depressive retreat, just as it also, eventually, intensifies (especially in the case of boys) the pull towards the most drastic of all pseudo-solutions – suicide.

In general, then, it could be said that one of the most common responses, on the part of 12–14-year-olds, to their physiological changes, to the stresses and uncertainties of school life, to the loosening of family bonds and to the confusion of feelings about themselves and where they fit in, is to seek out and try to immerse themselves in the vicissitudes, whether supportive or dubious, of group life. At this age, friendship groups are of the utmost importance. In terms of whether such groups are going well or badly, they could be said, for the majority, completely to dominate the experience of these crucial transitional years. Group experiences serve several functions, often somewhat different for boys than for girls and often with finely tuned distinctions between being just 12 or nearly 14. Part of the agony for 12-year-olds, for example, is that they are unlikely yet to have a firmly established group to which they feel they securely belong. Girls, in particular, in that they are more prone than boys to be caught up in the immediate hurly-burly of peer relationships, may suffer almost daily betrayals, disloyalties, exclusions, hopes and disappointments which are often very hard to bear or genuinely to forgive. By 13 or 14, however, such groups may have taken on a more constant, even tribal significance, of passion and intensity among themselves, and of hostility and indifference towards adults and their values. For parents, such hostility and indifference can be challenging and hurtful in the extreme.

In the most general terms, there are usually several groups in each school year, variously clustered together according to a vast range of subtle and changeable criteria: the broad ones of race, gender and class often reproducing society's own divisions and hierarchies. In any school year, however, there tends to be an in-group and an out-group (or groups), the "clever ones" and the "don't cares", the elite and the despised, the envious and the envied, and so on. There are the confident, pretty "pseudo-bimbos", as one teacher designated the attractive girls who presented themselves as empty-headed sex-bombs, while actually being among the most hard-working and clever in the year. "There are the pseudo-hard binge-drinkers, and the pseudo-self-harmers and show-offs," as one 15-year-old described her friendship group of the previous year, "but", she added, "things then divide into the workers and the others, and a lot seems to depend on whether your family has been warm *and* boundaried, rather than *just* warm or *just* boundaried."

Group membership, of whatever kind, usually, at root, functions as a sort of protective carapace, shielding the vulnerable young people from intense insecurities about who they really are as individuals, and where they belong as individuals. For all of them, the infinitely diverse presentations of 12–14-year-olds' allegiances and behaviour are but varying descriptions of how this troubled age group negotiates the transitional years towards a time of greater confidence in the kind of person they feel themselves to be, with what sorts of relationships, interests and aspirations. In the UK, most 12–14-year-olds will be in the first two years of senior school, and there is constant jockeying for position. There is a tendency to switch friends almost as fast as switching television channels. By the end of the third year (aged 14), as one teacher commented; "they tend to be becoming a bit more sorted, less challenging, draining and tiring, less insistent on negotiating every finer point of perceived justice or injustice." By this time, it is interesting that the fluidity of the 12-year-olds' groupings tends to have all but stopped, and comings and goings to any significant degree *between* groups is increasingly unusual.

Sometimes an individual can belong to more than one group, if he or she is careful. In such a case, it is quite common for the young person to be doing rather different things, in accordance with the respective group culture: behaving a bit differently, feeling a bit differently, dressing a bit differently, and speaking a bit differently. There may, for example, be one group at school and a different one at home, or elsewhere in the community. There may even be several different school groups among which such a person, especially if versatile and multi-talented, will move, though, perhaps, not entirely easily. Membership of several groups enables different aspects of the young adolescent's personality to be kept separate and yet to remain in contact with one another. As it becomes bearable for those aspects to be brought together in a more coherent way, so members of the respective groups may increasingly be allowed to integrate – social integration often heralding personal integration.

The grouping may be large, diffuse and generally benign – fans of a particular football team, for example. But it may be large, diffuse and generally malign, as in the case of the kinds of swarming, mobbing, jostling and marauding activities that go on in some inner cities, where people may be abused, attacked and mugged by a host of manic young teenagers whose group identity gives a protective licence to enact aggressive impulses which, individually, they would be unlikely to indulge. Whether the groups are large or small, the basic issues tend to be the same: membership is about a way of sorting out identity and negotiating separation, about daring to do collectively what would be proscribed individually. At a time when relationships with parents may well have become difficult or distant, group membership is a means of finding security with others who have something important in common, the basic commonality being to do with simply being in the 12–14-year-olds' maelstrom of experience. Aspects of character which are not yet acknowledged, nor, perhaps rightly, felt to be an ongoing part of a sense of identity, can nonetheless be bound together by the loose and invisible bonds of the group structure. Groups thus become safe places in which different parts of an individual's personality may be being played out, often parts which are felt to be difficult, or even impossible, to integrate in any other way at this stage.

In a group which roughly coheres in terms of style, race, fashion, music and class, there will very often be one member who is tougher than the others, one cleverer, one more sensitive, one rather rasher, one needier – each member, in a crude sense, standing for the tough, rash, clever, sensitive, needy aspects of each participant individual. The simplistic early stereotyping of the Beatles would be an example of distinctive, if mistaken, individual attributes being differentiated among group members: John, clever, rash; Paul, sensitive, creative; George, follower, less brilliant; Ringo, deprived. Whatever the truth of the stereotypes, the genius of the combination suggests that each represented essential elements of the others, the integration of which produced wondrous music.

In so far as everyone will, at times, feel, as Jane said, "completely misunderstood and a total outsider", the forces which bind this age group to an experience of similarity and belonging and therefore to safety, however uncertain, are, almost always, very powerful ones. Approval and status within the group become all-important. Exclusion is agonizing. The individual groupings often themselves become mini-societies of competitiveness and status-seeking, though usually not so intensely as to threaten the cohesion of the group as a whole. That is, these ambitious, omnipotent, disruptive, cooperative, dependent or destructive impulses on the part of the individual can, to some extent, be discovered, explored, lived out, experimented with and even, ultimately, reined in, within the relatively, often doubtfully, secure confines of the group structure.

Surviving this group life, however, is usually a great strain. Many feel the satisfaction of managing to maintain membership on the one hand, but, on the other, find themselves struggling with the burden of keeping up with who they are thought to be, or are wanting to try to be.

> For some reason the others found me marvellous, attractive, desirable. I felt I couldn't let them down and turned to diary-writing as the only place where I could really be myself and express my worries.

This comment of 14-year-old Anna would have surprised her friends, who believed her to be the charismatic centre of any party. But perhaps each of them would have harboured some private recognition of what she was talking about. For it is partly to combat the fear of isolation and the stress of keeping up appearances that friendships are formed in the first place. Those young people who have suffered particular abuse or deprivation in the past are especially prone to forming intense and seemingly unnegotiable relationships with a chosen peer group.

Despite the "safety in numbers" allure of much 12–14-year-old group participation, it is, nonetheless, striking that a number of young teenagers will long for the solace of one, single, special relationship and frequently confess to the paradox of "not really liking most of my friends". Such an admission points to the fragility and brittleness of many such group friendships and to the underlying need for some ultimately safe and trusted relationship which, at this stage, is often so intensely sought after; some proper alternative to the hitherto unconditional love of the family – a kind of love which feels, as yet, so unavailable, or unattainable, in the flux and fickleness of early adolescent turbulence.

In the second and third year of secondary or senior school, friendship networks do tend to be the centre of everybody's existence, but in a slightly more steady way than for the newly arrived and far from established 12-year-olds. Groups are felt to be the key to self-esteem, indeed, if going well, to making life worth living. Nothing is more important than social life, carrying with it the sense of elation if successful, or despair, if not. Yet, so often, much deeper feelings of distress and anxiety may be both masked and made manageable by the day-to-day crises of group membership. Gemma, whose parents separated soon after her thirteenth birthday, described how nothing mattered to her more than what was going on at school at the time. "Whether I'd snogged someone or even whether I had the right jeans to wear seemed much more important than the fact that my parents were splitting up." "Work didn't come into it at all," she continued, "it was school, socially, that counted. *Nothing* else mattered." What she did not realize until later was that it was the very fact that her parents *were* splitting up that lent particular weight and intensity to her group activities.

Group membership may mean that parents are dismissed by the hitherto most loving of children. The activities and shifting relationships of the group become paramount. Teachers too, even those respected because both tough and sympathetic, tend to be found irrelevant and embarrassing. A year tutor described his own experience:

> From regarding me as "God" in the first year, to thinking the "world of me" in the second, in the third, *everything* I did was wrong and despicable. It was not until the fourth year that I became accepted again as a teacher for whom they seemed to have any respect.

The pleasures of group life

School work also tends to be dismissed at this stage. It interrupts social life. The importance of continuing to study runs counter to the intense internal and external pressures of the age group, counter to the necessity of socially sorting out who the 12–14-year-olds feel they really are. Gossip prevails. It becomes an essential source of information, however distorted and unreliable (perhaps *especially* if distorted and unreliable) about the actions and intentions of the rest of the group or of the other groups. Whereas, in the past, parents would find the telephone monopolized as soon as school was over, leading to family tension and rows about phone bills, the advent of mobiles and texting offers the young uninterrupted access to each other's lives, a continuous hot line to the minutiae of moment-by-moment relations and tribulations of a kind that leaves many parents feeling entirely bypassed and redundant. Yet the seemingly endless appetite for conversation about each other's feelings, reactions and activities may often represent a way of trying out different aspects of themselves and of others' reactions to them. The subject of the gossiping, in other words, may, in fact, be nearer to experimental versions of themselves, and thus be inexhaustibly fascinating.

A further and related imperative is to go to *all* the parties. The absoluteness of this urge often has less to do with any intrinsic pleasure in actually being there than with ensuring that there has been no missing out on the collective and compulsive interest, for example, in who got drunk, in who got off with whom, in whether "the place was trashed", or in whether the ambulance was called. This is all very heady stuff, and it is not surprising that this is the time when the pressures to participate are most strongly felt, when the conflict between work and relationships is at its most intense, and when, as we have seen, the rows with parents about homework and leisure are at their most violent. Parents find limits harder and harder to set as the social demands intensify. Only a few months later on, perhaps at the beginning of the fourth year of senior school when approaching 15, the conflict has often to some extent been resolved: either to join those who are going to work for their exams, or to join those who are not. But at this younger age, body, clothes, hair, music, image, appearance, and above all, group acceptance, are the paramount concerns.

The potentially positive significance of such group acceptance should not, however, be underrated or dismissed. Naomi was sent to the headmaster of her large comprehensive because she'd been caught smoking in the school grounds. When he came out of his office to the waiting area, the head encountered six 14-year-old girls wearing identical jeans and boots. "We just wanted her to know that we were behind her," one of them said, smiling disarmingly. What the head was encountering was a group of girls who no longer felt as confused about their friends, nor about their own identity as they had when they first arrived in the school. Nor were they yet too worried about the pairing off into couples which would begin a bit later. This group of 14-year-olds was still relatively free of anxieties about exam pressures or the what-am-I-going-to-do-with-my-life worries that would follow. The pains and pleasures of the fighting, talking, sharing, subgrouping, excluding, regrouping, were all taking place in a relatively benign transitional space, one between what was, by now, being felt to be a rather more "holding" group structure on the one hand – one which may never be quite as tight or relatively carefree again – and, on the other, an increasingly restrictive family structure, now experienced, at least while the group mentality holds sway, as oppositional and disappointing or simply irrelevant.

Gangs

Not all 12–14-year-olds find their way into the sorts of groups just described, ones that, whatever the local gusts and storms, are fundamentally experienced as quite benign and providing structures in which a degree of care is taken one for another, and there is a considerable feeling of mutual concern as well as inevitable comparison and competitiveness. Very different are the kinds of groups whose attitudes and activities make them more akin to gangs. Very different, too, is the young person who finds him or herself a member of neither group nor gang, but socially on his or her own.

For, in contrast to Naomi's group of collectively challenging and individually supportive friends, other combinations of 12–14-year-olds may take on characteristics which are much less stabilizing and constructive, underpinned, rather, by patterns of tyranny and submission, of rebellion and even criminality. The members may have got together to express the destructive or hopeless aspects of their personalities, for the purposes of doing harm to themselves or to others rather than of doing good. All groups, at times, exert pressure on their members to do things that they would not have done as individuals. But this is a different matter from falling in with others *because* they seem to represent the more timid or vicious parts of the personality, and to reproduce an atmosphere of fear and oppression, so attractive to those who have been intimidated and oppressed themselves, whether at home or in the course of early school experiences (William Golding's *Lord of the Flies* is the classic description of this gang mentality).

"I couldn't count on my friends for anything but trouble," said Tony, looking back to how, as he described it, he was "seduced" into his 13-year-old gang.

> I started hanging around with this group…one of them had come up to me and said, "You're cool, we like your looks" and I just felt good for the first time in ages, and appreciated, and wanted to be friends. But they started doing things that I didn't really want to do – like bunking off school, skipping homework, taking drugs and getting into fights, and I found myself going along with it even though I felt it wasn't me.

We can see from Tony's account that he was already vulnerable – he didn't feel good about himself. Being accepted and having "friends" who, he thought, appreciated him, albeit only for his "hard" appearance, at least provided some kind of sense of a place to belong. Despite resistance, Tony found himself being pulled down a road that he neither valued nor wanted. He lived in fear of being caught out by his so-called friends, or of being found out by his parents and punished or rejected as a result.

Tony's gang, as so often, was dominated by a couple of older boys, leaders, who were felt to be charismatic, who "acted hard" and were already, as Tony put it, "into drugs and sex". These two offered the younger and weaker boys the possibility either of falling in with them and imitating their behaviour and attitudes, or of becoming intimidated victims within their own group. Any steps towards leaving the gang invited threats of harsh punishment. Tony managed to get out only when his older brothers told his parents, who had been too preoccupied by their own difficulties to notice Tony's.

They now realized both how unhappy and frightened their son had become, and the extent to which, out of fear, he had been lying to them about his activities. Several years later, Tony had difficulty in believing that the so-called leaders could ever have had such a hold on him. "They were really just victims themselves, and what's more, they haven't really changed. They're just the same now as they were then. In effect, lost."

Isolation

Tony's younger sister, Sandra, was among those who, for temperamental, practical or geographical reasons, can be much more isolated than the group or gang members hitherto described. I have been generalizing about the group-oriented culture of this age group but, of course, development runs at different speeds for different young people. Some stick closer to the family for longer than others, remaining identified with parents' values and attitudes and preferring not to break away or run risks. Others, perhaps those not living as part of a community, are not in a position to spend much time with friends. They may seek a different kind of companionship, for example, with pets, with books, with television and computer games, or even, privately, with toys that have usually been discarded by this age. This tendency towards solitude may or may not be something to worry about. If it happens by choice, it may represent a degree of self-knowledge on the part of the child in question about when he or she is ready to set forth and start making self-discoveries. It may, on the other hand, express excessive anxiety about growing up and an avoidance of confusion and conflict, a kind of retreat which indicates lethargy and possible depression rather than a more constructive biding of time.

Tendencies to isolation may also, as in Sandra's case, reflect a specific set of family stresses and needs. She was the baby of a family in which there had been a stillbirth three years earlier. She was small for her age and always a poor eater. Both she and her mother wanted her to remain "in the nest", maternally protected and safe from the "terrible dangers" which were perceived as lying outside the home. She preferred to stay close to her mother whenever possible, helping out, cooking, watching television and not apparently interested in anything in particular. Once she had transferred to secondary school, however, and the immediacy of her mother's involvement was necessarily diminished, she found herself lacking the kind of internal strengths so crucial to social survival at this age. Perhaps sensing her vulnerability, the other children would exclude rather than include her and she was cruelly bullied.

Sandra had started with a disadvantage: she was smaller than the other children. She looked different and seemed less robust and, as a consequence, missed out on an important qualification for group membership – sameness. It may be, too, that her mother, in wishing to shield Sandra from the more painful aspects of life, had actually handicapped her. For Sandra seemed to lack access to the resilience that she needed to make her way through what has, appropriately, been called the "blackboard jungle".

The long periods of listlessness and apparent boredom which many 12–14-year-olds seem to slide into, often involving hours of television or computer-based distraction, betoken a degree of mindlessness which parents usually find very upsetting. The bright and enthusiastic young 11-year-old seems suddenly to have "gone stupid". It may be hard to distinguish whether he or she is simply biding time before launching into the hurly-burly life that awaits, or whether these apparently addictive activities may, by contrast, signify a period of anxious withdrawal from engaging with the immediacy of adolescent turmoil, "the agitation of inexperience", as Pushkin so eloquently put it. Such withdrawal should always be taken seriously. For lassitude and mindlessness can equally be expressions of deeper depression, or of an avoid-ance of life – a mental state for which more than friendly tolerance may be required, such as help from a counsellor or therapist. A dulling-down of emotions also may indicate a fear of the more angry and destructive impulses and an anxiety about losing control. Yet these aggressive aspects of the per-sonality need to be known about, and it is precisely the relative safety of group interactions, whether in peer groups, in clubs or on the football field, that enable such aspects, to some extent, to be explored. Without these kinds of collective experimentation, the teenage isolate risks the negative sides of his or her character being not so much integrated as ignored and/or denied, with a resulting cost to self-knowledge and development, and with possible ill consequences in the future.

At school, Sandra was surrounded by people who were quite able to express strong negative emotions, but she did not feel safe enough to do so herself. Thus she never really learned to look after herself. It may be that her reluctance to eat was, as so often, linked with psychological difficulties of taking in experiences of which she was basically afraid, but which might have helped her to stick up for herself a bit more effectively. Or possibly, for her, biting and chewing were themselves a problem, stemming from a primitive fear of being in touch with early aggressive impulses which she sensed her bereaved mother would have found too difficult to bear.

Parents will rightly feel anxious about whether their children seem to have found their way to a relatively constructive group of friends, ones who will support the curious, courageous and creative sides of their characters, or whether the reverse may be true. For the groups and gangs of these early teenage years often have a lasting impact, specifically on confidence and self-esteem and more generally on attitudes, achievements and choices in life. Membership of a group or of a gang, or isolation from each, usually reflects characteristics of the 12–14-year-olds' personalities which can seldom be simplified as, "He fell in with the wrong crowd", or "She was lucky with her group of friends", or "He is simply a loner and is happy to be that way". Understanding the kinds of issues which underlie the complex allegiances involved may help to encourage the good characteristics and modify those which are not helpful to the respective development of each young person.

Much depends on the culture of the early years of any single person's particular school. As one teacher, jokingly, put it: "If you're a boy in my school, and you want to survive, you have to be middle class, very bright, brilliant at sport, and preferably Jewish." In another setting the "job description" of the survivor would look entirely different. When, in retrospect, a young person describes him or herself as having been "in disguise", as so many do, what they are identifying is the lengths to which they each had to go to find some kind of group membership which was sustainable enough to protect their idiosyncratic and fledgling selves from the individual and collective strains of living this life of transition.

To young people like Sandra, computer games, DVDs, the Net, etc. can be both a godsend and a danger. Chat rooms offer a form of virtual friendship which may be of profound consolation to some, for others exhilarating and risky, for yet others a source of interest and amusement, and for a few, frankly dangerous. Whether web relationships provide a welcome kind of holding and containment, or a temptation towards greater and greater excess, depends entirely on what the needs of the young person may be, and thus on what is the use to which the Net is being put, on what it is really for in each and every case: is it for escape; to combat loneliness; for experimentation; to satisfy curiosity, prurient or otherwise; to discover new experiences; to extend knowledge? When does curiosity become voyeurism, and sexual experimentation perversity? Like anything else, under certain circumstances, an interest may become an obsession, or a facility, say with technology, an addiction. The opportunities are there, and so are the perils. The tendency to deal with the emotional difficulties of young adolescent group-life by withdrawing is perfectly catered for by the growing culture consequent upon access to media of all kinds. In many cases, there is now an extraordinary array of technology to be found in the bedrooms of these young people – the television, the computer, the mobile phone, the Net. Though many would argue that this technology has its dangers, especially at this particular age, others would also argue that it enables the young to feel somewhat happier, better informed, independent and powerful.

> It can give people a place to retreat to, a kind of refuge from the life that they actually lead. It can also offer a support network and a feeling that there are people out there who do care about early adolescent difficulties and may think, for example, that you're attractive and funny, without all the problems of, say, what you or your mum and dad actually look like.

These are the reflections of a 15-year-old who was well aware of the mixed picture that the new technologies offer to the age group from which she had only recently emerged. She was thoughtful about the attractions, for many, of "being a complete expert in one particular field, and therefore more confident, especially among people who feel that that expertise is of value". She was also aware that such technology can be a solace to those who suffer from uncertainty and from difficulties in relating, particularly when group membership of one kind or another has not worked out for them. She commented on the comfort of seeing words on screen, of the sense of being in control of communication, and on the concrete form that that communication takes. The technology offers all sorts of possibilities to those who would not otherwise have had access to these alternative social groupings. Yet if abused, or drawn on indiscriminately, it also offers all sorts of worrying and time-consuming temptations, as well as equally worrying freedoms. These freedoms are very hard for parents to regulate or to manage in any easily negotiable way, especially when, as so often, the technical expertise of the young leaves the older generation feeling baffled and incompetent.

As we have seen, desire for inclusion and fear of exclusion are especially dominant in the 12–14-year-old age group. The respective groupings or gangings, whether actual or virtual, constitute, for the young teenager, social ways of seeking support for, and protection from, the very personal predicament of trying to become him or herself. An early casualty is very often that of shared family life as known hitherto, and parents often find themselves adopting a kind of "siege mentality" of sitting it out, until their offspring find their way back again a bit later on.

5

A Question of Identity
"Who am I?"

An aspect of the adolescent process being newly undertaken by 12–14-year-olds is likely to be one which involves feelings which they do not like, find painful, but, equally, would not wish to be without. Many of what seem the most bemusing, incomprehensible, destructive or disturbing aspects of adolescence can be thought of as ways of attempting, variously, to cope with, to bypass, to deny, to get rid of or to cover up unfamiliar and distressing experiences, often under the illusion that if they are not being directly felt or expressed, they are not really there.

What it feels like

More turmoil than is often realized attaches to the grief about leaving familiar things – the relative safety and certainty of childhood, for example, the known and the recognizable (including the known and recognizable shape of their own bodies). They are now compelled to move towards an unknown and less certain future, where every step of the way may feel both like a new ordeal and also, simultaneously, like a new adventure. At the heart of this predicament, though often presenting itself as quite the opposite, is the difficulty of leaving parents and home. To stress this difficulty may suggest an excessively rosy version of childhood. It is, of course, the case that to those for whom the early years have been unhappy ones, adolescence may offer a welcome alternative and childhood can be relinquished with scarcely a backward glance. It is, indeed, true that, for some, adolescence provides a second opportunity to engage with experiences and possible developments which were not available earlier, whether for reasons of health, loss, separation, or other setbacks and difficulties.

As we have seen, central to both the pain and the adventure of the 12–14-year-olds is the necessity of sorting out who they really are, as distinct from who their parents think they are or would like them to be. The question of physical and psychological identity becomes a central issue, and experimentation of every kind and on every front tends to become the main means of trying to sort out this central issue. For experimentation may both be a way of avoiding anxiety and also a way of trying to establish a sense of identity, however fluctuating and fragile. As we have also seen, the testing and challenging, both of adult authority and of themselves, and each other, tend to be at their most intense at this time. Thirteen-year-old Steven asked his mother one day: "Does everyone in the world think that he's the main guy?" This touchingly simple question was essentially about trying to understand himself. But it was also an expression of a dawning awareness of not being as special as he had thought he was: everyone else might believe themselves to be just as special, might even *be* just as special. If you lose confidence in that kind of specialness, how do you sort yourself out from the rest? The predicament becomes one of both wanting to be different and fearing to be different, or of wanting to manage to be different but within recognizable boundaries. The courageous thrusts forward are usually, at this stage, accompanied by anxious pullings back. Parents may feel perplexed by this apparent inconsistency, yet also perhaps recognize it, for it may mirror their own mixed feelings about wanting both to push their children forward to grow up quickly, and also to hold them back, mindful of "the day when they will be gone", and, in prospect, grieving the loss.

Rebelling and conforming

Early feelings may be stirred up in all concerned, ones reminiscent of the toddler who ventures just out of sight one minute, only to rush anxiously back to base the next; or of the mother who both wishes her infant weaned, and yet painfully regrets the loss of the intimacy of a baby at the breast; or of the father who feels the baby is driving a wedge between himself and his wife and seeks to regain the earlier one-to-one relationship. Such feelings will vary enormously according to the place the child has in his or her particular family. The 12-year-old who has two older siblings may experience a very different mother from the one the older children feel they have; likewise, the young teenager with brothers or sisters coming along behind. Their respective places in the family will often have much more to do with the course of these difficult years than is commonly recognized. Was their own birth, for example, too swiftly followed by that of the next sibling? Did they have to occupy the "good older brother" role for the younger children? Did they have to look after a depressed mother, or take the place of an absent father?

It is important to keep in mind the earlier childhood experiences, since the ways in which the stresses of adolescence are felt to be manageable or not are often closely related to the degree to which the impact of earlier difficulties has, in turn, been understood and managed in the past. Was, for example, the young child or parent able to express their feelings and, to some extent, resolve them at times of anger, grief or anxiety? Extremes of behaviour and generally excessive reactions to the normal stresses of adolescence – whether expressed as conformity or delinquency – are often rooted in previous problems or underlying tensions, the nature of which may never have been sufficiently acknowledged or addressed at the time.

Thirteen-year-old Annie had always been thought of as a confident and talented "model child". Shortly before a piano exam, however, she suddenly started to have panic attacks. She would run breathless and shaking from the room for no apparent reason. Three years earlier her little sister had been badly hurt in a car accident. Annie's mother had been deeply upset and depressed ever since, overwhelmed with guilt that she could somehow have prevented it. She was primarily looked after by Annie herself, who tried to "mother" her mother and cheer her up in continued efforts to be good and helpful.

In investigating Annie's panic attacks, it emerged that behind the good-girl exterior lay a terrible and longstanding fear of actually being very *bad*, indeed wicked; of having caused terrible happenings by her competitiveness and her desire to be her mother's only one, forever struggling (and necessarily failing) to compensate for any pains, imperfections or shortcomings by being "mummy's-little-angel", that is, by her "too-good-to-be-trueness". These competitive and destructive feelings were now breaking through her hitherto normally calm exterior, in the context of a further testing time – the piano exam.

Annie began to realize that she was somehow impersonating someone she was not; that she was covering up her own feelings of grief and guilt in order to conform to what she felt was needed and wanted by others. This was at the expense of her own sense of herself. Her own upset about her sister's accident and her irrational fears that she had somehow, jealously, caused it, had been insufficiently acknowledged, because her mother was, herself, too distressed by similar fears to be able to help her elder daughter. Having expressed some of these anxieties to a school counsellor – someone slightly removed from the immediate family situation – Annie had had a second chance to try to come to terms with her underlying unwanted and unfamiliar feelings. This new perspective involved her recognizing that she was not the person she had thought she was, nor did she now wish to be, since that degree of acquiescence had put the rest of her personality at risk.

Annie and Sandra had their respective unconscious motives for conforming. Others conform because, for whatever reason, they are happier that way – too timid, perhaps, to want to break away; too aware of parental distress should they try to do so; too content where they are; too identified with their parents' views and values to risk having their own. Each young person will have his or her own particular pace of development, and for some, the experimenting and the challenging does not happen until a bit later. For others, it may take covert and less recognizable forms.

Experimenting and testing: music, clothes, leisure

More common at this age, however, is the desire to test out everyone and everything. Discovering what is "not me" is a very important step towards sorting out what *is* me. It is often difficult for parents to understand that the fact that they themselves are being questioned and found wanting is only part of the story. What feels like rebelliousness, rejection and, occasionally, outright cruelty, may be an anxious expression of the need to find some kind of self-definition outside the known and tried relationships of the family. Adults find it hard not to assume critical and superior attitudes towards these efforts at self-expression. They may also be finding it hard to be the recipients of similar critical and superior attitudes now directed by their children towards them, the older generation.

Most 12–14-year-olds are moving from being defined by, and defining themselves as being the son or daughter of their parent or parents, to seeking to know who *they* are, as distinct from those parents. Concerns about the relationship between being merely a son or daughter and being a separate self become very insistent. For this reason, early adolescence is often the time when searching questions are raised about natural parents. Adolescents in their families of birth struggle with tolerating and integrating (or rejecting) the clues and pointers that they encounter every day.

Adopted children and their adoptive parents face particular difficulty when the question "Who am I?" is being asked. They have far fewer, or even no, clues or pointers from their adoptive parents as to what kind of person they might be or become. For children, the opportunity to question, accept or refuse their parents' personality traits is an important part of the development of their own identities. But adopted children have to cope with being ignorant of what is felt to be crucial information about themselves, and to accommodate the idea of at least two sets of parents whose respective legacies remain confusing and opaque. This situation can feel undermining and lonely for children of all ages, but perhaps for young adolescents in particular. They may find themselves going to greater and greater extremes in their need to prove and test themselves and, especially, to prove and test their adoptive parents' love for them, in attempts to find some kind of secure and meaningful basis for their own sense of self, and some parental model to which they feel able to relate.

Where experimentation is concerned, taste in music is often the first casualty of shared family life, expressing, as it does, the *different* sounds and the *different* group allegiances of a *different* generation. Perhaps, in cultural terms, for adolescents it is music that, above all, defines the distinction between themselves and their parents. For the enjoyment of popular music is a reflection of a youth culture of a very contemporary kind, racially mixed perhaps as never before, vibrant, responsive, loud, immediate, and quintessentially expressing the sounds, lyrics, rhythms and beats of the new drum of the new young generation. Music is a central part of an initiation into life to come; a crucial aspect of shared identity and group bonding; a crucial aspect, too, of a fundamental means of differentiation from adults of a kind which often unites otherwise very disparate peer groupings. Fifteen-year-old Soraya described herself and her friends: "At 12, listening to music was more to do with identifying with a certain image than with enjoying or knowing about the music itself." She recalled her dad liking a CD she had just bought. Sheepishly she reported that, as a consequence, she herself had never listened to it again: the assertion of generational difference in taste in music far outweighed the significance of her own independent preferences.

Choice of clothes is usually allied to choice of music – both potent statements of difference and belonging, of group identity and ritual behaviour. The need for differentiation from parents and authority figures, the seeking after new mentors and role models, is a necessary but risky business, the uncertainty of which is often expressed in the tendency, even necessity, to wear the *same* clothes as others, though perhaps with subtle, scarcely detectable differences. These passionate concerns with the details of trainers, haircuts, or how laces are tied express, in part, an almost slavish attention to shared style, an informal uniform of belonging, and an attempt to minimize actual difference. But they also, in part, express anxious and enjoyable grooming and preening (no less so among the boys than the girls) as manifestations both of an overwhelming interest in their own changing bodies, and also of the deeply serious commitment to group life already described.

There may often be seemingly incongruous manifestations of the desire to define generational distinctiveness by dressing differently from parents. In one rather unconventional family, the father characteristically wore dirty jeans and shoulder-length hair. His fourteen-year-old son, Pete's, response was to iron his own jeans, wear a white shirt and tie, lurex socks and plastic sandals. The effect was just as intended – his father was uncomprehending and furious. He took his son's dress code as a personal attack, unable to distinguish what felt to him like an act of pure filial hostility from a desperate attempt, on his son's part, to find a way of defining himself as separate from his father. This father's unconventionality made it all the more difficult for his son to establish his own generationally combative style than for many of Pete's contemporaries.

While the young people of this age group, and often well beyond, can emphasize distinctiveness in their own "style statements", they are, however, usually powerless in affecting their parents' choices. Embarrassment about parental dress, or, for example, choice of car is often at its most acute during these years. Many a parent will have had to accede to dropping off their youngster round the corner (even in the pouring rain) lest the dreaded exposure to friends' scrutiny actually take place.

The shared impulse, in terms of self-expression and leisure pursuits, tends to be to try to live on the edge – an edge differently defined for boys than for girls. Boys' increased physical strength and hormonally fuelled energy often encourage them to test their own daring and prowess to the limit. Their sporting activities may take them to the end of their physical endurance. At this age, the important issue is often the process itself, not necessarily the goal. But activities such as basketball, karate, football, mountain biking, skateboarding, for example, can become a passion and the rewards, in terms of social kudos and inclusivity are great. Being "built" and good at sport is a huge asset for the boys, whether among their male or female peers, just as being overweight or physically nondescript can be a terrible liability.

The sportsmen reap a very considerable harvest in terms of self-esteem. Admired and envied, they seldom endure the torments of bullying, nor the misery of marginalization. It can, however, also happen that ever-increasing urges towards greater physical feats represent anxieties about hidden senses of failure or inadequacy in other areas, the danger signals being when accidents begin to occur regularly, or when training becomes an obsession rather than a pleasure. On the whole, though, success in sport provides supportive and constructive channels for the indomitable energy of many young adolescent boys. Without it there may be all sorts of much less socially adaptive outlets for the kind of restless, aimless casting-about for a focus of tension or aggression that besets some boys of this age. However, the challenges and excitement expressed in, and contained by, sporting activities can, for those in a more destructive frame of mind, fuel quite other, much more delinquent, enterprises: collective muggings, thefts, breakings and enterings, running in marauding and adrenalin-fuelled packs, engendering fear and anxiety, and darkly enjoying an omnipotent sense of challenge and control, as their young legs carry them triumphantly towards escape from their adult pursuers. In yet other cases, excessive consumption of alcohol or of drugs, especially the smoking of cannabis, can represent a retreat from, or a defensive alternative to, these various manifestations of, by turn, ebullient energy and physicality or omnipotent opposition and criminality.

Yet it may also be that, in some states of mind, apparently daring deeds and athletic feats have less to do with excitement and danger, whether licit or illicit, or with engendering anxiety in others, than with a need to discover the relationship between aspiration and realization, with an insistent drive towards reality-testing, towards checking the boundary between hopeful ambition and actual possibility. Parents need to have the confidence to let their children run a degree of risk, to make mistakes and suffer the consequences, but always within a firm boundary of known and negotiated limits, however often they may be challenged or disregarded.

Among the girls of this age, the "edge" also tends to be expressed through the body, but, in their case, by sexual acting-out rather than by competitive physical activities. "What do you want?" screamed the distraught mother of 14-year-old Rose, who had been sleeping out with a group of friends for several nights without telling her parents where she was. "To do what I want, without *you*," was the furious reply. "Well, you can't. You have at least to ring us up." The negotiation was eventually and painfully concluded. If Rose stayed out she would always let her parents know where she was. If she asked to be picked up they would come for her. If she wished to walk after 11 p.m. it would never be with fewer than two other friends.

Going to the limits

Both Rose and her friend Emma spent their years from 12 to 14 courting danger. They described, in retrospect, what a strain the seeking for status, the urge to *be* someone had been, whether through sex, drugs, piercings or general recklessness. They said that they had somehow believed that there would be "guardian angels" protecting them from the terrible risks that they so insistently and carelessly ran. They spoke, too, of what a relief it was to feel able, at 15, to acknowledge their true "guardians", namely their parents, and sometimes to bring their friends home with the recognition that communication between generations was, after all, possible, at least to some extent.

Emma described how awful it had been "snogging older boys" when she was 12.

> I didn't want it, I didn't like it. I found it horrible, at the same time exciting, and I was supposed to want to do it. When I tried smoking and drugs I found them absolutely disgusting, but being grown up meant doing these things which I hated and looking as though I was enjoying it.

Rose and Emma were both painfully discovering something about what it meant to be themselves by experiencing what *wasn't* themselves. They both recounted how, at the time, they would attach themselves to glamorous older boys who represented direct challenges, and also alternatives to their parents. They sought status, flattered by attention and by boasts and false promises ("I can get you into clubs free"; "I can get you a job any time"). Because girls, as we have seen, mature slightly earlier than boys, at this point they are often going out with partners two or three years older than themselves, thus finding themselves involved in activities, sexual experimentation in particular, which tend to be far more precocious than that of their male peers – both thrilling and terrifying.

Emma and Rose described their girlfriends as either like themselves, "vamps", as they put it, or as trying to prolong the kind of self-protective stance of remaining "tomboys". Each type was, in its contrasting way, putting off the dangerous moment of engaging with the complex question of what femininity meant to them personally by identifying with caricatured aspects of the female or the male worlds. Both of these strategies, they reflected, might have had something to do with trying to find alternatives to the main available model of femininity – that of "mother". But both these strategies also reflected very familiar ways in which girls either avoid, or prematurely engage with, what puberty thrusts upon them. These ways are often only temporary and, as with Rose and Emma, have more or less passed by mid-adolescence. But, at the time, parents tend to feel tested to their limits – as they are meant to be.

Parents' response to the challenge

Parents often feel that they are the ones who suffer all the anxiety and not the young person in question. In many instances this is true, and exceedingly burdensome. For one of the main psychological mechanisms of this age is that of projecting into others unwanted or uncomfortable feelings as a way, temporarily, of reducing internal tension and conflict. Thus, anxious and excluded, parents will often be suffering *for* their offspring. They also have to find ways of being able to bear *not* knowing what is happening much of the time; ways of engendering in their children the secure sense that their home remains their haven, albeit so often abused; ways of being able to face how much they might well be hurt and worried if they knew what their children were actually doing, and of not being too frightened about that, nor feeling too personally rejected; ways of understanding that the "drama queen" or the "Mr cool-and-detached" of today is still the frightened child of yesterday and of tomorrow, in danger, at any moment, of feeling completely misunderstood and cut off from base.

Crucial to parents' capacity to manage any of these taxing undertakings is the recognition, on their part, that straight prohibition is likely to arouse either secret rebelliousness or phoney submission, while excessive tolerance usually promotes a search for some kind of limit on the part of the 12–14-year-olds, however far that may have to take them. In this respect, past patterns of family authority may be very important. There is usually a world of difference, in terms of self-regulation in young adolescent behaviour, between having experienced authority that is based on love and respect, and a more authoritarian approach that is based on distrust and the inculcation of fear. The latter threatens the young with being found disappointing, with an imputation of failure, with falling below standards, even with loss of love. Thus when parental anxiety is expressed through distrust, threats and prohibition from early on, the effects can be the reverse of those intended. For the insistent drive towards self-development and self-definition will often cancel out promises extracted under duress and encourage acts of sometimes astounding duplicity. Despite the provocations and difficulties, many parents do, none-theless, find ways of supporting the arduous process, on their children's part, of building their own internal structures of licence and self-restraint. At this stage, there may be many setbacks and disasters in the process, for what is parentally forbidden is usually far more attractive than what is cautiously allowed.

One 15-year-old boy reflected on the possibility that neither he nor his younger brother had joined the large community of 13-year-old binge-drinkers because their parents had never made alcohol a no-go area. Both boys had been used, since they were quite young, to a watered-down glass of wine on formal occasions. "Or perhaps," he added, "it was a helpful attitude because we felt that our parents knew each of us well enough to give us a bit of rope and not be on our backs all the time."

By contrast, one young graduate from an uneducated, but very ambitious background, having just gained a first-class degree at Cambridge, recalled his toil through scholarships to private schools, lower and higher school exams, university entrance and final university exams. "That's the last thing I'll ever do for my father," he said. And only then was he able to begin the belated, and therefore more painful, task of sorting out what he wanted for himself and who he really was, apart from being a clever boy and a successful son. He had been helped by his father's ambition for him, but it had also come at a price.

6

Running into Difficulties

The previous chapter described the normal testing, differentiating and limit-finding that often, though by no means always, characterize relationships between parents and their 12–14-year-olds in the course of the central enterprise of this age: establishing who they are in their own right. Any one of these routes to self-discovery may extend into more worrying behaviour if it leads beyond what is tolerable to the young adolescent or to the parent, the school or wider community. It may find expression in behaviour or in states of mind that are antisocial, despairing, delinquent, obsessive, seriously self-damaging and destructive, or in some sense outside reasonable or rational control.

The urge to self-discovery is, as we have seen, centrally to do with love and loss – the primary emotions involved in separating from parents. The process almost inevitably entails conflicts, grief, disappointments and anxieties. But although it is characteristic of this age to go to extremes, worrying problems may arise when ordinary and appropriate exploration gets out of hand. The difficulty often presents itself as one of not knowing where to draw the line, or how to recognize the crossover point from "extreme" to "excessive", be it in the area of computer games, of food, drugs, alcohol, sex, cleanliness, homework or whatever.

This is an especially difficult area for parents since it usually stirs up powerful feelings. Anger, shame, guilt or distress often make it hard to see that such abuses, whether directed at the young adolescents themselves, at the parent or the outside world, may also be important forms of communication of which the true message may have become quite obscure.

If the communication aspect can be grasped, some kind of understanding and containment of the problem may be achieved. The difficulty is that, by its very nature, this more extreme behaviour tends to obliterate thought and meaning and to focus, rather, on an axis of action and reaction. The greater freedoms, independence and responsibilities that young people begin to acquire at 12, however much desired, can often make problems and decisions seem overwhelming. Luke revealed:

> I can get so depressed. Part of me knows that I can get out of it really, but I also don't want to. I sort of enjoy it. I suppose I really want my mum to come and look after me.

Feelings such as these can be so intense that the only thing to do seems to be to act, or "act out", as it is sometimes called. The "acts" are responses to inner pain, often related to external and understandable stresses. But just as often they appear not to be attached to any obvious source. Many 12–14-year-olds don't know why they feel the way they do and then feel worse *because* there is no apparent reason. Often the world seems suddenly and unexpectedly bleak. Equally suddenly a small change may transform everything.

After a particularly intense outburst of bad temper, 13-year-old Carol admitted to feeling depressed – she had no idea why. Nothing was going right for her and she felt really bored, alienated from her friends and generally miserable. A few minutes later the post brought a special magazine that she had sent off for. Her face lightened and she completely cheered up. "I think maybe I was just disappointed because my mag hadn't arrived." What had seemed a bad case of existential angst swiftly yielded to ordinary measures of frustration and gratification.

Much more significant is when it is not the magazine but the friend who doesn't arrive as promised, or who turns out to be spending the day with someone else despite a prior arrangement; or when the young person isn't invited to a party that everyone else is going to. The capacity, at this age, to deal with these kinds of setbacks and disappointments depends on a number of things which are closely related to how serious a risk there may be of damaging or destructive behaviour as a result. First of all, as already stated, puberty affects different children in different ways. Some experience a sudden and dramatic increase in their feelings of anger and aggression as well as of passion and desire, and, as a consequence, suffer impulses which they find very hard to control. For others the situation is much less intense and disturbing. The capacity to manage these new feelings, of whatever intensity, has a great deal to do with the degree of communication and understanding about emotional states and their expression already existing in a family. Some children feel that their parents are able to think about and respond appropriately and wisely to childlike struggles to communicate. They have learnt to expect their feelings somehow to be "held", mentally, at times when they have not been able to do so themselves. As a result they will, over time, have had the opportunity to develop that same capacity in themselves. They will be able to think before they act, in turn to "hold" extremes of feeling, without lashing out, collapsing or being otherwise overcome by them.

This early capacity on the parents' part for forbearance, receptivity and responsiveness to the troubled states of early infancy, is often again sorely tested in young adolescence. The children's impulses are, as we have seen, particularly strong. One way of dealing with them may be to try to get rid of feelings into someone else, either to get others to feel them instead, or to communicate just how horrible the feelings are. If parents are still able to acknowledge, tolerate and relate sympathetically to these, by turn, adult and infantile explosions of rage, love, despair, dependency, they will stand their children in better stead for establishing their own limits. As young people they will feel additionally strengthened or supported in the holding of their own line if there is felt to be a measure of parental trust in their ability to do just that. Enormous self-respect accrues from the knowledge that parents basically believe in their children and, when it comes to it, will back them in times of adversity.

This confidence in parental support should not, however, be confused with a family position that is so tolerant that anything goes. Just as unhelpful would be the family position that is so intolerant that blind loyalties, distrust and prohibition obscure more subtle differentiations about right and wrong. Children who have become used to such parental extremes, in whichever direction, are often exposed to particular difficulties in controlling their behaviour and impulses because they have no discriminating internal rules (or "guardian angels") to fall back on. In the face of especially lenient parents, they may become excessively guilt-ridden and hard on themselves, struggling both with their need to indulge feelings and with their self-hatred in so doing. Yet in the face of over-harsh parents they may become excessively punitive themselves, and vengeful towards others, with unthinking responses of the "eye for an eye" variety.

It is the parent who is able to differentiate between, for example, need and greed, between what really matters and what doesn't, who is prepared to hold out for what he or she believes is right despite a fight, who can help to engender in the children a similar capacity. It is extremely important to try to maintain this capacity in adolescence, even if it seems ragged at the edges at times.

Families in which parents find it difficult to control their own impulses, or ones in which excesses or inconsistencies of whatever kind are a characteristic of home life, often find that their young adolescent also has difficulties with self-control – having either too much or too little. Similarly, excessively rigid and authoritarian parents who tend to see things in very polarized ways may, inadvertently, encourage their children to go to extremes, while believing that what they are doing is simply setting limits.

It is between the ages of 12 and 14, when the bodily changes are so dramatic and the consequent turbulence in emotions and relationships so new, exciting and frightening, that these internal controls become especially severely tested and, as a result, pose particularly demanding challenges both to self and others, to family life and school life above all. It is not surprising that the peak age for "acting out" of all kinds is 14.

Stealing

Susan, aged 14, had been caught stealing. The incident came to light when her teacher questioned her mother about the inappropriately expensive clothes and jewellery she was wearing to school. The teacher felt concerned rather than punitive because she knew that Susan had been unhappy for some time and had discussed with her whether or not she would like to talk to a counsellor about her behaviour. The teacher's attitude encouraged Susan to share her feelings. The recent theft from her grandmother of money with which Susan had bought the clothes and a ring was more serious than in the past when she'd taken minor items or small sums of money from her mother. When Susan said she had also taken the blame for a friend's recent theft, the teacher realized that Susan had probably *wanted* to be found out, which was why she had worn the stolen items so ostentatiously at school.

She put this to Susan, who agreed with her teacher's surmise and then tearfully poured out the story of the last few years. It had begun when her mum's boyfriend had unexpectedly moved in two years earlier. Her own father having died four years before that, Susan now felt that she had lost both her parents and she wasn't central in anyone's life any more. Her moodiness around the house and her frank sexual competitiveness with her mother for the boyfriend had raised threats to put her in care. Susan acknowledged that she was pushing her mother to the limit and trying to drive a wedge in the relationship with her new boyfriend, but said that she felt she couldn't help it. When her mother had turned to a boyfriend instead of to her, to help get over her grief at the loss of her husband, Susan had become despairing – no one could understand or bear *her* needs. She felt very angry and abandoned and had considered suicide in a vengeful kind of "then she'll be sorry" way, but "For some reason," she said, "I ended up stealing instead."

The teacher suggested that mum and her boyfriend come in to school and that they all talk about it together. Her mother was upset to learn how very unhappy Susan had been. She had attributed Susan's bad behaviour to jealousy of her boyfriend and had hoped that she would grow out of it. She said that Susan had not grieved for her father much at the time and that she thought she'd got over it – acting as a tower of strength towards her mum, rather than showing any great distress herself. Mum described herself as feeling too overcome to notice much at the time anyway.

It became possible to talk not only about Susan's jealousy, which was certainly strong, but also about the much deeper emotions of underlying grief and loss. Susan had initially tried to overcome these emotions by looking after her mother as the only way that she felt she could get looked after herself – that is, she did for her mother what she herself needed. But when the boyfriend took over that role Susan felt she had nothing to offer. She described competitiveness, anger and even hatred towards her mother, the very person whom she also loved so profoundly. This unaccustomed hostility made her guilty and terribly confused. Moreover, just at the point when she herself was sexually maturing, her mother had found a new boyfriend. Susan explained how she felt really put down by that, and anxious about whether she would ever be found attractive or have a boyfriend of her own.

The stealing could thus be thought of as a way of getting back from her mother and grandmother something she believed she had lost and should rightfully be hers. It could also be thought of as a way of acquiring things relating to the very area she was anxious about – items of femininity with which she sought to boost her "image" and attract boys. The stealing had a third function for Susan. She hoped that punishment would relieve her feelings of guilt – not about the stealing itself, but about her aggressive impulses towards her mother and her mother's new relationship.

The stealing was, then, a distress signal – one which Susan had had to escalate when the initial salvoes went unnoticed. Fortunately, in this case, her teacher was sufficiently understanding to "read" stealing for what it was. Having been able to talk over her feelings of rage and guilt, Susan no longer felt compelled to act in such a way as to invite a punishment that would be quite irrelevant to the so-called crime.

Stealing can be taken to stand for a whole range of designated antisocial acts, ones with which parents of 12–14-year-olds so often find themselves involved. The challenging, "naughty", or even criminal, behaviour often arouses punitive impulses, and sterner discipline is felt to be the solution. But there is usually an underlying reason for such behaviour, one based in conflict or distress. Understanding what the problematic behaviour may mean, and being able to sort out the appropriate response, is difficult for a closely involved parent when feelings are running high. Often the views of a thoughtful third person, like the teacher in this case, will be helpful in knowing the best way to proceed.

Drinking, drugs and other problems

Underage drinking, and experimenting with substances, whether solvents or drugs, is another difficult area which a large number, even a majority, of parents reluctantly find themselves having to face: in terms of their fears for their youngsters; of what they feel about the illegality and the excess; and of what they are going to do about it. As with stealing, and all too often closely related to it, this kind of problem may have a number of meanings. Having some sense of what consuming alcohol and taking drugs may signify in relation to a *particular* child is much more helpful than a cover-all response based on anxiety, prohibition and possibly ignorance.

As we have seen, the onset of adolescence may be felt to be "too much" for many young people. Drinking or taking substances are two of the many forms of relief and/or escape. For this age group it is very difficult, especially now that drugs are so easily available, to resist the temptation to avoid the worrying, unpleasant or imperfect aspects of life by inhabiting altered states of mind, ones in which both the self and the world may, temporarily, look and feel much more manageable and enjoyable. Drinking to excess or drug-taking is often based, though perhaps not consciously, on wanting to avoid stress and conflict: especially, as we have seen, if that stress and conflict stems from feelings of unhappiness, inadequacy or inferiority. This is an increasing predicament for the boys of this age, as the girls become more assertive, confident and powerful. It may also, however, be to do with an adolescent yearning for new experiences, with the belief that such experiences will lead to important self-discoveries. In addition, there is the strain of not wanting to be different from the friendship group who are beginning to experiment with drugs and alcohol as part of an oppositional stance in the face of parental strictures. The use of drugs and alcohol can, if moderate, be relatively benign, and certainly enormously pleasurable. To excess, however, it can, like many kinds of incipient self-harm, criminality or delinquency, provide an omnipotent source of excitement about, for example, being reckless, powerful or insouciant, about the pseudo-maturity of feeling grown-up and independently minded, without having to go through the painful process of acquiring a sense of real strength and judgement by slower and more ordinary means. Defying normal social rules often offers great social status among other young adolescents, and taking drugs or getting drunk, in particular, play into the desire to appear "hard" and "laid back" about issues which others of this age may find much more complex and agonizing.

A helpful parental response to this usually alarming world might initially be simply to know the facts, to have some sense of the actual dangers and effects of different drugs, to be able both to recognize worrying signs and to distinguish between situations in which there should be legitimate alarm rather than a permissive attitude.

14-year-old Sarah, who had been smoking her older sister's cannabis for over a year, described watching a television programme with her parents on teenage drug habits. Her mother had commented, "What must these parents be like? If that was you, we'd know." It had never crossed her parents' minds that either of their daughters knew anything at all about drugs. Or, perhaps, they had never allowed themselves to be aware of the signs. Whatever the reason, this ignorance on their parents' part was, for the girls, in the short term, a source of relief, tinged with triumph. Later, however, when their habit escalated to harder drugs and eventually came to light, Sarah and her sister found themselves without any basis of family understanding or support, either for their addictive behaviour or for the difficulties which underlay it. The family exploded in rage and grief. Only much later did the painful process begin of discovering and facing the reality of a fundamental lack of genuine family communication and emotional reciprocity, a lack which had lasted over many years.

Drinking or experimenting with drugs *may*, by contrast, also be part of a rather more constructive self-exploration, and a way of questioning the conventions of family and society – "How can you think puff is so terrible but

poison yourself with fags and alcohol every day?" This characteristic adolescent challenge may characterize those who are not so much self-destructive or
escapist as going through a period of challenging rules as a necessary step
towards accepting or adapting to them. They are seeking, in other words, to
come to conclusions based on their own experience rather than on what their
parents tell them. Indeed, many of the arguments that 12–14-year-olds will
mount with their parents are really arguments with their own selves – wanting
the saner and more reasonable part of the personality to be supported and
understood, despite protest. As such, these arguments are statements of
conflict – one part of the self desiring the very discipline that the other part is
busy flouting. The role-reversal is interesting, though often felt, by parents to
be exceedingly provocative. Young people characteristically become very
hard line and disapproving about their parents' habits while fiercely defending their own right to behave in similar ways, as if asserting a kind of carica-
ture of parental attitudes, in reverse.

The drug culture is a terrifying one for any parent of young teenage
children; the feared progression from "puff" or "weed" to harder drugs and
the danger of getting AIDS through sharing needles. Many parents will have
learnt, to their cost, that "prohibition" really spells "invitation" and that, in this
area, as in so many, their children cannot, in any straightforward sense, be
controlled. Beyond the necessary explanations of the risks and dangers,
parents have to think about what their own attitude really is. They need to be
mindful of what their own "drug" behaviour may signify to their children –
tobacco, alcohol, sleeping pills, tranquillizers, even overwork. And they have
also to reflect on what drugs may mean for each of their own individual
children, in terms of the variety of motives and vulnerabilities described
above.

Mrs Green rang her friend in a panic. Her husband had come home unexpectedly during the school day and had found their 14-year-old son,
Nicholas, smoking a joint with a couple of friends. What should she do?

> I know he's a bit of a tearaway and we had to be pretty heavy with
> him about cigarettes when he was 12, but he said he'd stopped
> smoking – and anyway this is quite a different thing.

She said that she had forbidden him ever to touch the stuff again but wasn't at
all sure that he would abide by that: "He's become so devious. I can't really say
I can trust him at all." Two months later another mother rang to complain to
Mrs Green that Nicholas had been supplying his year with dope. "Where", she

demanded, "did he get the money from?" It turned out that Nicholas received a substantial daily allowance. While consciously appalled at the idea of their son taking drugs, his parents were, at the same time, unwittingly providing him with the financial means to do so, without addressing the impossible temptation that this might arouse in such a boy, already an established smoker at 12.

More commonly, parents increasingly find themselves, equally unwittingly, and, on discovery, despairingly, funding adolescent drug habits either through the covert stealing from purses or wallets that goes on in many households, or by outright threats and violence. As drug habits take a grip, the idea of negotiated financial allowances tends to go out of the window and, instead, parents find themselves confronted with the intemperate blasts of frustration and desperation of the young person whose substance abuse has got out of hand. Under such circumstances, increasingly prevalent in the 12 to 14 age range, parents find themselves terrorized or helpless. Certainly, outside support is necessary, though probably not deemed acceptable until the prospect of irremediable damage and failure pulls some back from the brink.

It is, then, a rare young person who, like Annie, explicitly raised her wishes and anxieties with her parents. Annie had become friendly with a group of 14-year-olds who regularly took acid trips. She wanted to try herself but was worried because one of her friends had recently had a very frightening experience during a trip. She took the very unusual step of asking her parents what they would think if she tried.

Like many areas of behaviour and experimentation among 12–14-year-olds, the culture of drugs tends to be a secret one, largely conducted behind closed doors and usually well beyond anything that has been admitted to parents – the secrecy itself, of course, being an important source of attraction and pleasure. Degrees of involvement with drugs vary enormously at this age. Some will be forming a habit, others only rarely trying things out, yet others will be going along with it as a ticket to social inclusion, and a remaining few will have little access or experience.

Annie's parents had had quite a permissive attitude towards her older brothers' occasionally smoking marijuana and they had a general, but rather vague, sense of the nature and effects of "acid" or "LSD". In response to Annie's question, they decided to find out more about the subject. What they discovered caused them considerable concern and they passed on to Annie the information they had acquired about the specific dangers and possible disturbing consequences of this particular drug. In the course of this discussion Annie decided that, despite group pressure, she would resist the temptation and felt relieved to have her parents' thoughtful and informed position to support her.

Eating disorders

Drug-taking certainly falls into the category of what is called self-harm. Although drug-taking often involves both boys and girls alike at this stage, in this case, unlike alcohol, it tends to be the boys who find it harder to exercise restraint, especially, as we have seen, when faced with the intellectual and/or sexual superiority of the girls, or the sportive achievement and 'street cred' of other boys. An eating disorder, on the other hand, is primarily, though not exclusively, a girls' problem. Being self-conscious, as well, possibly, as self-righteous and health conscious, is an ordinary aspect of being adolescent – the prerogative of knowing better and being superior. Many 12-year-olds of either gender, for example, become vegetarian at this age, driven by a variety of motives. On the one hand, they may be claiming the moral high ground from their parents by adopting positions that they would argue to be ethically, politically or economically preferable. While these arguments are often, in themselves, coherent and sound, the motives are also, just as often, under-pinned by quintessentially adolescent anxieties about, for example, contami-nation, or about cruelty, guilt and aggressive urges that arouse the unconscious protective imperative of reining in and controlling. By contrast, the underlying motives may be constructive and reparative: as in the wish to preserve and restore "mother" earth by restrictive environmental measures. In other words, however conclusively the conscious position may be rationalized, it may also be deeply embedded in unconscious preoccupations, hence the power and recalcitrance of the political or environmental positioning for the young person concerned.

To an extent, food-faddishness can be attributed to needs for differentia-tion and individuation and can, more or less, be accommodated in the normal course of things. But issues around food often take on a more troubling tone than the well-argued stands on, for example, being vegetarian, vegan, macro-biotic or whatever. Most 12–14-year-olds feel dissatisfied with how they look – the boys no less than the girls. But whereas puberty for a boy tends to increase height, build, strength and energy, contributing to their sense of manliness and potency, for a girl the picture is very different. For them puberty brings a filling out the bodily contours, a roundedness of hips, a developing of breasts and a general weight gain. Their upward growth spurt tends to come earlier than that of boys and so, for many, puberty tends to mean growing "out" rather than "up", a situation which fills many 12-year-old girls with fear and hatred of their new bodies, anxiety about being fat and determination to go on a diet. For many the problems are exacerbated from external sources: by the ever-increasing availability of fast food, for example, and the extending range of well-publicized and frequently encountered dietary advice. This all too recognizable picture may be only the beginning of many a tormenting story.

The loss of the previous body shape, and the unwilling change to the new, also represents a clear shift from being a child to being a woman and the ending of the choice to be boyish, or tomboyish, which many girls make as preferable to being part of the world of girls and mothers. The fact that it is still fashionable for women to be thin makes things more difficult. At this stage many girls begin to be worried about the amount of food, and the kind of food, they eat in ways that may become seriously problematic. Many begin to be picky, then to restrict, then to starve. Others begin compulsively to overeat and then to binge, and then to binge and purge, either by taking laxatives or by vomiting. This behaviour may be a reaction to, or a compensation for, how bad they feel about themselves, or a response to the loss of, or absence of, things they still feel they need but fear they no longer have the right to. In a very simple sense, aversion to food (anorexia) can be a way of exerting control over a life that is feared to be becoming unmanageable in the ways already described, or has been experienced, until now, as being in the control of others (especially the mother).

The unconscious determinants of the refusal or excessive control of food are complex indeed, and usually fall far outside any cajoling, common-sense or irritated parental response. They belong, rather, in a very mixed unconscious picture of separation and individuation, of ambition and self-determination. For while excessive food restriction may, in purely physiological terms, put a stop to ordinary sexual development, it is also inexorably harnessed, variously, to feelings of guilt and lack of entitlement, and also to a sense of covert triumph, to a need for evident and surpassing achievement, to a fierce battle for betterment, and to a relentless quest for a (deluded) version of physical perfection. Any and all of these felt imperatives are, at root, indissolubly linked to anxiety about the tie with the mother, about ordinary intellectual and physical growing up, and about distorted and competitive expressions of that "growing up" – moral, intellectual and personal. All such conscious and unconscious determinants represent early adolescent problems writ large.

They require understanding, vigilance and, almost certainly, professional advice.

So, too, do the eating disorders which tend towards bulimia – the compulsive-eating end of the axis. These difficulties may represent either a feeling of emptiness, absence and irremediable loss of something felt to be necessary for the ongoing development of the self, or that things are hopelessly out of control, or both. Binge-eating may be an attempt to fill the internal "hole" or to regulate the fear of absence and to stop it before disaster strikes.

Such eating difficulties tend to represent the obverse of one another, but each can be regarded as flagging up fundamental difficulties of self-esteem, self-worth and self-evaluation. Whether the problem is that of over- or under-eating, the young women are all involved in a considerable amount of torment and self-hatred, the beginnings of which are now so dramatically evident in the 12 to 14 age group.

Inevitably, taking in too much food, or refusing food, or developing food fads and weird diets, almost always stirs up strong reactions in parents, particularly in mothers, who feel either that they are being rejected, or that they cannot provide enough of the right things, in the right way. They may find it hard to restrain irritation, even fury, about apparently irrational and exacting food fads. They may also find it worryingly difficult to know when to allow a daughter freedom in the area of food restrictions and when to be properly concerned and to seek help elsewhere. For a mother will often become aware that, in relation to her own body and to her own relationship to her maturing daughter, food cannot be a neutral topic. Unless a lot of receptive thoughtfulness is brought to bear on the situation, it can become an agonizing battleground for other things: "I hate my body and therefore I hate myself" is often expressed on the part of the young teenager by some version of "I hate you and everything you have to offer me."

Promiscuity

Like eating disorders and drugs, promiscuity and the associated dangers, whether of sexually transmitted infections and diseases, or of pregnancy – long recognized as a problem for older adolescents – are becoming more and more common in the younger age group, especially among the girls. Promiscuity, at this age, is clearly a self-destructive and risky way of expressing a variety of feelings – whether of fear, of the anxieties of separation, of loneliness, self-hatred, desperation, need for love, desire for danger, or premature impatience for "adulthood" – without the intervening uncertainty of making one's painful way through the adolescent years. These days, promiscuity and risk-taking, unprotected sex carry with them the specific, horrifying and increasing danger of HIV, of chlamydia, of syphilis and many other alarming and even deadly outcomes. As we have seen, sexual experimentation can, sometimes, be part of young people's efforts to find out who they are, what they want and how they feel. If, however, such sexual experimentation takes the form of sensual relationships with many partners, without any apparent intimate feeling or contraceptive protection, probably there is some kind of underlying desperation, deprivation or bravado going on – in each case, perhaps, expressing a cry for help, or a bid for attention, whether the "child" consciously knows it or not. Again, understanding what may underlie such behaviour and how it relates to the parents' attitude to sexuality, to the current state of their own relationships, to the degree of their genuine mental and emotional availability to their young teenagers, is of utmost importance.

Any of the activities and preoccupations of this age group may, of course, be taken to excess at any time. The reasons are usually similar: distress about feelings that 12–14-year-olds do not understand clearly, nor believe that anyone else could do so; attempts to avoid having such feelings; convictions that people who could have helped in the past are no longer able to – namely the parents. It is hard for parents to accept that they may, indeed, be felt no longer to be worth talking to, especially so for a single parent. What may be unexpectedly helpful is simply the recognition of what these processes are about and the ability, up to a point, to let the young be themselves. Being themselves is likely, now, to be very different from who their parents are or from what the young think, perhaps erroneously, their parents want them to be.

In these difficult areas it is important for parents to be aware of their own states of mind at that same age. Although the context may seem dramatically different, being able to be in some kind of dialogue with their own 12–14-year-old selves, with the feelings of being young teenagers in a hostile adult environment, can help enormously in understanding both the emergent adolescents and the nature of their own reactions to them. For parents may often, unexpectedly, come across long-buried aspects of early experience that colour their attitudes and influence their behaviour towards their young. They may find themselves, in a rush of shocked recognition, relating to their own teenager in precisely the ways their parents did to them, ones which they so berated at the time. Remembering how they felt then may help to avoid simply repeating old conflicts, possibly battles. They may, as a result, be able to free their children to find more enlightened ways of expressing themselves, encouraging independence within a sense of secure and caring limits. They may equally, on the other hand, find themselves too much in tune with the reactions of their 12–14-year-olds and lacking the necessary parental distance which, although a major irritant between generations, may also offer the teenager firm and helpful boundaries. A parental claim to be "best friends" with their young teenager seldom inspires confidence.

One can see how many of the problems which become serious in mid- and late adolescence may have their roots in this 12 to 14 age group. One can see, too, how important it is to understand what is going on at the time, lest the eating fads become disorders, lest the feelings about emptiness become ones of pointlessness and despair, lest the confusions and difficulties become forms of avoidance and mindlessness, lest the self-hatred become serious self-abuse, where self-mutilation, drugs, sex and numerous other forms of self-destructiveness develop into the myriad ways that unhappy and confused adolescents find to harm themselves and to distress others.

7

Life in the Family

As we have repeatedly seen, for children, letting go of those who have been the centre of their world for so long is a very painful business. The cruelty or casualness with which that letting go is often done tend to mask deep underlying distress. The person who until then *has* had most of the answers cannot now be looked to for solutions to, or opinions on, areas of anxiety and confusion that may feel more pressing and frightening than anything that has gone before. They cannot be looked to, not only because, in reality, they are not able to make everything alright in the way that they have in the past, but also because to try to do so is to maintain an intimacy which is now felt to be variously threatening, intrusive or unwelcome. One sad and disillusioned 14-year-old reflected on his disappointments, "I realized they couldn't get me through life. I had to do it by myself."

The problem for the 12 to 14 age group is that they feel a pull away from parents (particularly from mother) and back to them *at the same time*, and the various solutions they find to cope with this fact are neither very firm nor very long-lasting. They find the inside conflicts hard to sort out, but they also become driven by outside, social pressures to behave in ways which they may not really feel ready for. These muddles are often evident to parents in the young adolescent's characteristic desire to be allowed to remain childlike – having things done for him or her (room cleared up, breakfast made, etc.) while at the same time wanting the privileges of adulthood (staying up late, being given responsibilities which, when unfulfilled, can go overlooked or else risk enormous rows).

14-year-old Jason's mother was perplexed by her son's constant complaints that she was never in. She asked him why it was so important for her to be at home when he himself was always out with his friends. "That's quite different," was his reply. "I just want you to *be* at home whether I'm there or not." What is often difficult to recognize is that it is precisely the mother-taking-care-of-child-at-home that frees the young teenager to explore areas of life with friends elsewhere. The security of feeling that his mother was at home was, for Jason, a precondition for further experimentation of a kind which felt very different from the heady, but worrying, licence dubiously enjoyed by some of his friends who could not reliably count on any attentive parental presence.

For the first time, then, these no-longer-children and not-yet-adults are likely to be going through a lot that parents don't know about – and necessarily so. When parents start encountering a new secretiveness and reserve, it becomes painfully clear that the young people are definitely entering their own world. Their hopes and fears, anxieties and conflicts, will increasingly become ones with which they will often be struggling with friends who are in the same boat, or, possibly, alone. For a parent, to make it clear that he or she is available as and when the young indicate that they wish to confide may be the best that can be done. A parent may be both wanted and yearned for in his or her old role, as the one who is "there" and responsive at home, yet felt to be useless, thick, embarrassing, redundant or intrusive, as the one who, in other more social circumstances, has to be tolerated or shunned. Some days, or even at some moments, it will be one, on other days and at other moments the other. Parents may constantly have to remind themselves that one of the central tasks of this age group is to separate, and there is no predicting the timing, the ways or the means in which this will be done.

Parents may find themselves thinking, "They've stopped needing me or talking to me in the way they used to, there's no point in my making an effort to be in after school or during the evenings." The child's response, like Jason's, may well be, "But I want you to be there *in case* I need you." The point is simply to provide a reasonably stable background or base from which the child can go out into the world. Finding the right balance between being experienced as intrusive on the one hand, or uninterested on the other, is very problematic. The likelihood is that it is quite important that parents be made to feel that they have got it wrong, whatever they do. It is part of the struggle to separate and to bear the pain of it, that what is being separated from has, at times, to be felt to be not worth having anyway. Parents are left with the feeling of being useless and helpless a lot of the time, and the finely honed capacity to engender such feelings is a particular speciality of 12–14-year-olds. A little later, or perhaps only a long time later, the adolescent or young adult and the parent or parents may have found a way back to a relationship that functions on a different basis, but at this early stage it is a painful experience for parents both to be actively devalued and also, perhaps, to be discovered as not being what their children thought they were, or even what they themselves would like to have been.

Parents separating from children

Wounded parents are having to think hard about the unfairness of being ignored or harshly judged and wrong-footed at every turn, while also having to face actual deficiencies in themselves which they might otherwise prefer not to see or want to think about. The patterns of discipline and response which have become well established within the family group may now be altered, disrupted and tested anew. Old and familiar patterns of authority are often found to be provocative or unworkable. Indeed those patterns, themselves, may now be revealed to be limited, unjust or obsolete.

This age group presents a fundamental and almost always difficult challenge: for parents have to be prepared to change too. They have to be able to deal with the adolescent in themselves, perhaps alarmingly and thinly covered over with what they took to be their mature, adult selves. Often the children will provoke rows to find out what their parents are *really* like. Often, too, no one much likes what is revealed – least of all parents themselves. The young may come across, or uncover, hypocrisy and double standards. Parents may have to acknowledge envy of their children's youth, beauty and opportunities. They may also have to face their own inability to let go or to separate, to allow the young their freedom. For many this involves the painful acknowledgement that the "child" is no longer "theirs", in the way that the pre-pubescent child was felt to have been. Up to now parents have made the rules, taken the decisions, organized the activities, and generally been the person turned to for approval, love, advice and comfort. All of a sudden, at 13 or so, the young person is felt somehow no longer to belong to that same parent – and this is extremely threatening to many parents, arousing fears of being surpassed, left behind or no longer needed. They may even have to struggle with quite unexpected and disturbing possibilities, like the arousal of their own sexual desires towards their now physically maturing children.

Although seldom experienced consciously or explicitly, such unwonted and unwanted feelings may lie behind the intensity of some parents' reactions and prohibitions – seemingly irrational rules and strictures often ill conceal-ing more basic possessive and emotionally charged responses, the fundamen-tal nature of which the parent may be quite unaware. There may, in other words, be many confusions, inconsistencies and about-turns that make the adolescent's task the harder unless everyone concerned can honestly reflect on what is going on. Here a thoughtful partner or friend with whom to share the stresses and incomprehensions can be enormously supportive and reassur-ing, and can help to contain some of the parents' own "adolescent" responses, even outbursts.

Separation and divorce

In a new family where either, or both, "parental" adults may have had children by former partners, or be beginning another young family of their own, the expression of feelings on the part of the 12–14-year-olds may take very extreme forms, especially ones of blame and recrimination. As we have seen, these young people naturally tend to see things in very exaggerated terms. They may well view the replacement partner through excessively biased eyes, usually because he or she is *not* the real parent, but occasionally because the new partner may be felt to be better than the natural parent – a situation which, not surprisingly, arouses guilt and confusion.

More usually, all the hostile feelings that the young person has, but is frightened of expressing, towards the natural parent may be directed towards the replacement. One parent thus becomes exaggeratedly good, with qualities perhaps valued quite beyond his or her actual worth, while the other becomes excessively devalued, criticized and sniped at on every occasion. The splits may be felt to be, indeed are, like those in the fairy stories – the wicked witch and the good fairy, the envious stepmother and the kindly father. There is a tendency towards this kind of exaggerated split between good and bad in any family with children of this age, for dividing experiences and people into extremes of idealization and denigration can function, as in infancy, as a way of evading potentially more complex and demanding feelings of ambivalence and therefore of uncertainty. It is thus not surprising that such polarized feelings become all the more absolute when actual separation has occurred or is threatening. This kind of polarized and absolute attitude is especially hard for parents and new partners, since so many raw nerves are likely to be touched. But it is important not only to take very seriously the hurt, and there-fore often very *hurtful* feelings of the young person, but also to try to moderate them where possible, making efforts not to intensify them either by ignoring the distress or by adding fuel to the flames.

Ron was 14. His mother, though separated for five years, nonetheless felt very upset when her ex-husband began to live with a girlfriend, Joan, and she couldn't resist criticizing Joan at every opportunity. Ron had mixed feelings to start with. He was a bit relieved that his father was no longer on his own and that therefore he, Ron, didn't have to feel responsible for spending time with him and cheering him up. But as time went on he felt crosser and crosser. His mum was upset, his dad was completely taken up with the new relationship and, worst of all, they were talking about having another baby. He started telling his mother that he was beginning to dislike Joan, and then that he actually couldn't stand her, and, finally, that he absolutely hated her.

When he stormed home one night, announcing that he completely refused to eat any food Joan cooked for him, his mother's feelings were very complicated. At one level she was delighted that Ron would not eat "her" food. But she also realized the danger of supporting him in that position. She felt it was too extreme, in that Joan really seemed quite nice and was obviously trying to be good to Ron. Was Ron wanting to please his mum? Was he feeling jealous and displaced by Joan? Was he furiously needing a reason to reject his father and doing so by rejecting the girlfriend? Or was he angrily expressing feelings about Joan which he was not able to admit to having about his mother? It may have been a mixture of all of these things and more.

Contrary to her own impulses, Ron's mum decided that he should be encouraged to go on seeing his father, but perhaps not always with Joan there as well. It seemed to her that the most important thing was not to put at risk a relationship which was basically very important to Ron at a time when he was reacting quite violently to a number of aspects of the adult world, but to try, rather, to support him and his dad and to see how things could develop from there. Part of Ron's difficulty may also have been to do with the fact that, seeing his father happy with another young woman, not his mother, stirred his feelings of grief about the actual separation five years ago. It is very common in this age group for feelings about loss and grief to be re-aroused in this way, and often very painfully.

Such was the case with Mary. A few months before her fourteenth birthday she started crying inconsolably at the least provocation. Her friends were worried about her and, appropriately and impressively, told her form tutor. Until then Mary had been a model student, an apparently popular and happy girl who was expected to do brilliantly in her exams when the time came. To start with it was thought that she was both upset about her closest friend leaving the school and also worried about the next year, when exam work proper would begin, for she had already expressed anxiety about fulfilling her parents' academic expectations.

In conversation with the form tutor, Mary poured out profound grief and distress about her parents' divorce six years earlier. The tutor had heard from Mary's mother about the separation and had been told that Mary had taken it very well at the time; in fact, she had hardly seemed troubled by it at all. She had, apparently, immediately begun working hard and excelling at everything. Mary's present distress belied the optimistic and understandably defensive picture her mother had presented.

Because she was worried and frightened for her daughter, Mary's mother had needed to minimize the impact that the separation had actually had and to focus on her daughter's strengths and successes rather than on her vulnerabilities. Mary herself had sought to avoid her own distress, and the extra worry that that would cause her parents, by devoting herself to school work and to other achievements. But it seemed that the superficially much less important loss of her friend had revived her upset in the context of new school worries. These worries were also now given an extra meaning. For it turned out that Mary had always harboured the irrational fantasy that if she did really brilliantly, she would be able to bring her parents back together. The fear of failure threatened her with having to face the fact that this was never going to happen.

Brothers and sisters

In households where there has been a loss or separation, even ordinary problems may become especially highly charged. But in most families, general strife will often accompany early adolescence and outbursts will tend to occur over issues which have hitherto been reasonably smoothly negotiated. The flashpoint between brothers and sisters is frequently over matters of, for example, differential pocket money, bedtimes, household chores, or attention given.

In these contexts, there is felt to be a world of difference between 10–11-year-olds' relationships with older or younger siblings and those of 12–14-year-olds. At 12, sensitivity to rights and prerogatives often suddenly changes. Relationships with younger brothers and sisters may have muddled along, with not much attention being paid, for example, to the value of money, or to effort expended on bothering to calculate the exact percentage more allowance that Johnny should have by virtue of being three years and four months older than Susan. At 12, however, parents may encounter situations in which, as in Jake's family, the washing up may be done not only begrudgingly, but also now according to an elaborate system of putting a price on each plate, saucepan and item of cutlery. Jake's parents despairingly described him as claiming new exemptions and privileges, and, among many other areas of trivial hair-splitting, doing elaborate, though pointless, calculations as to how to outdo his younger brother (who didn't much care) and his older sisters (who were by now more generous).

The major contests tend to occur with younger brothers and sisters rather than with older ones. The 12–14-year-olds become suddenly sensitive to differences of status and preferment which they feel should naturally follow from their superior years. They often become contemptuous of their younger siblings and, by turn, competitive with, and dismissive of, the very care and attention on the part of parents which they themselves are so busy rejecting. They also begin to feel able to participate in the world of older brothers and sisters and not be the child any more. Lawrence described this new sense of privilege in relation to his older brothers:

> When I reached 14, if anyone picked on me, my brothers were there to support me. Tom would take me places – out to work with him. His mates would say, "What are you bringing him along for?" Tom would say, "If he's not coming, I'm not coming." It was great.

At this age the whole complex arena of rights and status suddenly becomes hard fought and hard won.

The more equal, albeit quarrelsome, relationships with younger brothers and sisters now tend to change and a new kind of tension gets introduced into the more familiar types of conflict. What had been mildly teasing behaviour is suddenly experienced as severely provocative, and often mutually cruel. The threshold of tolerance becomes much lower and the tendency to hit back or even hit out, is much greater. Parents are often driven to despair by this new aggressive edge to the hitherto manageable competitiveness and arguing. Bearing it as "just a phase", which is what it usually is, can feel excessively testing at times. The battles do not seem to trouble the young people themselves, who often feel more comfortable with the increasingly flexed muscles or barbed tongues than the adult world quite appreciates.

It is not unusual for 12–14-year-olds to find themselves unexpectedly faced with a new baby in the family – a last child for parents who respond with a new pregnancy to the running of their own biological clocks, and perhaps, too, to the pain of their youngest suddenly becoming adolescent. Older teenagers may welcome this event as mobilizing the beginnings of their own latent parenting feelings and impulses. A younger adolescent, on the other hand, hitherto the smallest in the family, may be deeply put out by having to give up that special position, and may respond with versions of acute jealousy that can often take quite extreme forms of withdrawal, premature escape into alternative "worlds" or, more dramatically, in the case of girls, with their own pregnancy.

On the other hand, the appearance of a younger brother or sister may relieve a situation, familiar to many, in which the young adolescent has found being the smallest very hard and has cast him or herself in the role of the loser in the family. Tracy described herself as coming to some stark conclusions when she was 12.

> It was a nightmare really. My older brother and sister seemed to be fine but I hated everything. I was so ugly and useless. I used to read the problem pages in magazines to find someone weirder than me. At home I just shut up – became completely silent for about two years. I just had a blank mask. My mum would say, "What's wrong?" "Nothing," I would say. Or, "What are you thinking?", she would say. "I don't know." I felt that being the youngest was so limiting. But also I suppose it made things safe. Maybe it was my family keeping together and their expectations that kept me going. Lots of my friends didn't really come through.

The "rough justice" approach of the earlier years is often peremptorily swept aside at this stage and demands for preferential treatment become more strident. Parents find themselves with major diplomatic problems on their hands, both wishing to confirm the adult strivings of their child as now being distinct from the needs of younger brothers and sisters, yet also having to keep in mind the more infantile collapses and dependencies which do frequently occur. Lawrence, now 20, spoke warmly of his parents' capacity to offer him "a certain amount of rope to experiment with", but in a context in which "I knew there was a firm point at which a line would be drawn, however much I objected to it at the time."

The eldest of Lawrence's three older brothers, Tom, had had a less fortunate experience: "I think adolescence hit Tom very hard and unexpectedly," said Lawrence.

> Adolescence was new to him but it was also new to my parents. They were quite an isolated couple, living just outside our small town, and they didn't have much sense of what went on. Being treated differently from all your friends is an acute embarrassment and breeds deceit and trouble – at least it did with Tom. I think Tom suffered terribly because the rules in our family, at that time, were so different from other families. Dad's idea of being a father was to work all the time and bring in the money. He missed out on my older brothers. With Tom, Dad's way of sorting things out was to give him a thick ear, but that changed a bit as we younger ones came along. That way of dealing with problems went out the window. I think he learnt from his experience with Tom, but Tom suffered as a consequence.

Sharing with other parents

Lawrence's account touches on many important issues, particularly, perhaps, the difficulty of reacting to the stress of the new experience of 12–14-year-olds' boundary-testing with measures that are neither too punitive nor too restrictive, nor too frighteningly permissive. In this context, a sense of relationship with the "rules" of other families of young adolescents may be of great importance. Although the chance to talk to other parents at the school gate is now past, at this next problematic stage a sense of connection on parents' part with the main issues in the young adolescents' world is of enormous value. Establishing acquaintances, or even friendships, among parents of similar aged children may offer very significant and helpful insights, as well as much-needed support.

If there are some loosely agreed ideas about reasonable bedtimes, about how late the not-so-young ones sleep in during the day, about pocket money or allowances, parties, drinking and so on, it can be a great deal easier for parents to feel that shared boundaries can be established and adhered to. For the young adolescent, too, there may be a sense of relief that there is some kind of limit-setting going on which has been commonly arrived at by a group of parents, rather than being a set of uniquely unfair crosses for them to bear – throwing up endless individual grievances. A characteristic "skill" at this stage, on the part of many 12–14-year-olds, is the ability to split the adult world and divide it against itself, particularly parent against parent, parent against teachers, or parent against other families. In a situation where the position is, "I'm the only one who isn't allowed to stay over", head-on confrontation can often be avoided by means of a concerned, though not too intrusive, parental network of agreed limits and licenses, by contrast with each contentious point being repeatedly fought out on individual battlegrounds.

Conclusion

Most 12–14-year-olds, and their parents too, are taking exciting and difficult steps forward at this time. Young people are finding their own unique ways of negotiating the strange process of discovering a sense of authenticity, which may turn out to be very different from what they or their parents expected. Each step carries with it not only its own losses, ones that are often difficult to adjust to, but also its own gains, ones that may not be as apparent at this time as they become later on.

This is an age that is increasingly dreaded by parents, and increasingly marked by intense suffering on the part of the youngsters. Few would say they loved being 12, but they might concede to some enjoyment by the time they were 14. This book has been about that complex and fraught transition, the struggle from one stage to the next. The results of the struggle can be both enriching and damaging. At best, the weathering of these turbulent years, through resilience, understanding, tolerance and honesty, may often expand and deepen relationships between parents and children, enabling each to separate, to grow, to change and to establish the basis for lasting friendship and mutual respect.

Further Reading

Burningham, S. (1994) *Young People Under Stress: A Parent's Guide.* London: Virago.

Madaras, L. (1989) *What's Happening to my Body? – Boys.* London: Penguin.

Madaras, L. (1989) *What's Happening to my Body? – Girls.* London: Penguin.

Mayle, P. (1993) *What's Happening to Me?* London: Pan.

Patterson, C. and Quilter, L. (1991) *It's OK to be You: Feeling Good about Growing Up.* London: Piccolo.

SCODA (Standing Conference on Drug Abuse) (1992) *Drug Problems: Where to Get Help.* Available from SCODA, tel: 020 7928 9500.

Helpful Organizations

Adfam
Waterbridge House
32–36 Loman Street
London SE1 0EH
Tel: 020 7928 8898
www.adfam.org.uk
Advice for families facing problems with drugs or alcohol

Anti-Bullying Campaign
185 Tower Bridge Road
London SE1 2UF
Tel: 020 7378 1446
www.bullying.co.uk
Advice for victims of bullying and their parents

Brook Advisory Services
421 Highgate Studios
53–79 Highgate Road
London NW5 1TL
Tel: 020 7284 6040
Helpline: 020 7617 8000 (24 hours a day)
www.brook.org.uk
Confidential advice on sexual health and contraception for young people

ChildLine
45 Folgate Street
London E1 6GL
Tel: 020 7650 3200
Helpline: 0800 111 (for children and young people)
www.childline.org.uk
Confidential 24-hour helpline for children and young people

Eating Disorders Association
103 Prince of Wales Road
Norwich, Norfolk NR1 1DW
Helpline: 0160 362 1414 (Monday to Friday 9 a.m. to 6:30 p.m.)
Youthline: 0160 376 5050 (Monday to Friday 4 p.m. to 6 p.m.)
www.edauk.com
Information on all aspects of eating disorders

Exploring Parenthood
Latimer Education Centre
194 Freston Road
London W10 6TT
Tel: 020 8964 1827
Parents' Advice Line: 020 8960 1678
Advice on parenting problems from newborn to adult

Families Anonymous
Doddington and Rollo Community Association
Charlotte Despard Avenue
London SW11 5JE
Tel: 020 7498 4680
Helpline: 0845 120 0660
www.famanon.org.uk
Support for families of people with drug-related problems

Gingerbread Association for One Parent Families
7 Sovereign Close
London E1W 2HW
Tel: 020 7488 9300
Advice Line: 0800 018 4318 (Monday to Friday 9 a.m. to 5 p.m.)
www.gingerbread.org.uk
Support for single parent families

Lifeline for Parents
101–103 Oldham Street
Manchester M41 LW
Tel: 0800 716 701 (helpline Monday to Thursday 5 p.m. to 9 p.m.)
Information and support for parents

Parentline Plus (formerly National Stepfamily Association)
Tel: 0808 800 2222 (helpline 24 hours a day)
www.parentlineplus.org.uk
Information and support for parents

Release
388 Old Street
London EC1V 9LT
Tel: 020 7729 9904
Helpline: 0845 450 0215
www.release.org.uk
Information on drugs, the law and human rights

Samaritans
The Upper Mill, Kingston Road
Ewell, Surrey KT17 2AF
Tel: 020 8394 8300
Helpline: 0845 790 9090 (24 hours a day)
www.samaritans.org.uk
Confidential emotional support for people experiencing feelings of distress and despair, or contemplating suicide

Turning Point
101 Blackchurch Lane
London E1 1LU
Tel: 020 7702 2300
www.turning-point.co.uk
Services for people with complex needs, including drug and alcohol misuse, mental health problems and learning disabilities

YoungMinds/National Association for Child and Family Mental Health
102–108 Clerkenwell Road
London EC1M 5SA
Tel: 020 7336 8445
Parents' Information Service: 0800 018 2138
www.youngminds.org.uk
Campaign to improve the mental health of children and young people

Index